NAKED TRUTH

NAKED TRUTH

Ieshia Leverette
Editor: Amani Jackson

Lady Leverette

DEDICATION

I dedicate this book to my little sister who is braving the storm, fighting her way to a better life I pray she finds. Hope is not lost for her and she will only be as lost as she chooses to be. The support and resources are standing in front of her, and anyone else in need, but it will truly be up to her and you to utilize them.

This is for every youth in the hood who speak with fist and rage. Understand you are worth more than they will ever tell you. Knowledge is not only what they are willing to share with you. Find it in books beyond any school's curriculum. It is guarded in the wisdom of our elders. You'll stumble upon it in your day to day activities if you are vigilant enough to notice it when it reveals itself.

This is for those of us who had to make a way with little to no resources or support. I know it may not seem like it, but none of us were placed here without the tools to survive and thrive.

For every young girl who feels her hips, thighs, breasts, and vagina are her greatest weapons-stop selling yourself short. You have so much more power by simply being a woman. Your presence, what you mean to communities as a nurturer and healer, our instinct to protect and guide is invaluable.

Dear young man, block out all vile deceptions railing at you any contradiction to your worth and rightful place. You are the leader, the head and not the tail. You were created to protect and direct. Don't allow society to make you doubt yourself. Regardless of the obstacle, the victory is yours. Keep your head to the sky and your eye on the goal. You belong at the top. The road may not be paved, there may be many detours, and predators are surely lying in wait for you, but never stop. So much, for not only you but your present and future community, depends on your purposed manifestation.

I'm rooting for you. But never allow anyone to root for you harder than you root for yourself.

Parents, if you have missed all the stories, news articles, movies, speeches, pleas, or mantras telling you how much your children need you, hear it now. You are irreplaceable. While many may step in to bridge the gap, you are necessary. Your children come from you. Parenting is an experience in and of itself. Let your children heal what is broken in you. I've heard so many people admit having children saved their lives. You can do it.

To the aunts, uncles, older siblings, cousins, grandparents, and great-grands who stepped in when they were needed, we can never say thank you enough. You paid the price when it was not yours to pay and poured into a child not your own. You refused to see an innocent torn from family and placed in the system. You are the pure and lovely example of family. Thank you for being selfless, loving, reliable, and present.

CONTENTS

Intro 1

Dna 5

West Coast Shorty 15

Home Sweet Home 19

Elberon 27

Pillars 49

Money Moves 63

They All Come Crashing Down 89

Toledo 95

Taking The Hood To The Suburbs 103

New Beginnings 147

Melvenia 149

Elithia 151

Michael Eaton A.k.a. Herc 157

Denise A.k.a Deedee 163

Death Of Jackson 168

INTRO

Greatness is forged from mastering the good, the bad, and the ugly within. When people heard whisperings of this project they asked, "How can you possibly write a book about your life, being so young?"

"Easy." I smiled. I can write this book because my age is one thing, but my experience is beyond my years. My life has seen me do things and has taken me places many haven't. I find myself inspiring all ages, ethnicities, and economic backgrounds. Life happens to us all. It is so freeing and healing for someone to speak with you candidly and supportively instead of hiding behind pomp and status. Under it, all are festering wounds eating us alive since they are not being addressed. When you have truly lived life, and met as many people as I've met around the world, you learn that everyone has a story. In hearing them, you'll find the story itself is not as important as the process of the journey. Life's lessons are in those details.

After a few years of sharing my story and hearing how it impacted the listener, I realized the potential of so many more people needing to hear it. Not in ten, twenty, or thirty years when I've lived more. But now, right now. They are hurting and healing now. Wandering aimlessly for a kindred spirit; feeling lost, defeated, judged, and hopeless. My story is relevant now. Plus, I want to release what is inside to make room for the next chapter and story to follow. Tomorrow is promised to no one. People often say the grave is full of brilliant ideas. It's full of healing encounters which were never had also. Mine won't be one of them.

Writing this book was liberating and therapeutic. So many emotional ups and downs occurred because I faced and closed gaps in my life story that I hardly knew existed. I am a transformed woman with a story that will resonate with many. I may not be proud of everything I've done, and I wouldn't have done many of them given a second chance, but I have no regrets. Do we always wish we could tell that young person about the consequences that would be standing before them? Do we wish we could be someone else or walk someone else's path because of the hand we were dealt? I was once that person, but now that I've lived through this much of my journey, there is no other life or story I would have preferred to have been blessed to encounter.

I believe I have been blessed with a gift which attracts people from a similar background. Sharing a common ground allows me to be a blessing in their lives via mentorship and guidance. Looking from the outside it's easy to want to be someone else or have their circumstances over yours. However, to know their story would make your story feel meniscal compared to the trauma they have experienced. No matter who the person is, I notice their past pain in their actions and their eyes. We don't realize how true it is that the eyes are the windows to our souls. They say what we won't. I can tell you right now, I'm happy to have had my story after seeing what others have been made to withstand.

I don't think I've met a person who has not experienced some level of trauma in their life. Rather, trauma is distinguished by classes: upper, middle class, or lower. Everyone's interpretation of life differs according to perspective. There is no perfect life and I will never portray to be perfect, but I will always be open about my story. If it helps one person feel empowered it was worth the time to tell.

Through writing this book, I've been overwhelmed with compassion and a desire for healing those in my life. My mother and father may have not been my primary caretakers due to their drug and alcohol addictions, but no matter what your love is never abandoned. You may be angry and resentful, events may have led you down a path less desirable, yet when you really begin to heal you realize love, forgiveness, and progress are requirements. Your parents, or anyone who you feel disappointed or neglected you, have had their own

INTRO

life-altering traumas. It's always so easy to point the finger regarding their shortcomings, but creating a space for understanding and communication goes a long way to bridge the gap to healing.

I am an overcomer. I am of an environment and statistic. Still, I chose not to let it define who I am. I didn't do it by myself. I had the initiative to discover and attract the right people into my life and it made all the difference.

This is one of three memoirs I invite you to delve into. See yourself in the pages and plant whatever seeds of growth you find in my experiences. More than anything, relax and enjoy getting to know me for who I was, how I became who I am, and who I aspire to be.

DNA

Make no mistake, very few places compare to the real Cleveland. I'm talking from Elberon to the border of the suburbs in Cleveland Heights. I'm not talking Tower City with its tourist-attracting shops or upscale restaurants and the wealthy bliss of Gates Mills, Pepper Pike or Bentleyville. No, the heart and soul of the city knows nothing about the entitled, segregated segments of society who can't even relate to the day to day at ground zero.

There wasn't a single morning I woke to the beautiful melody of a bird's song, floating down to me from a nest in a tree by my bedroom window. Crickets didn't sing lullabies to escort children off to sleep where I'm from. Those things only happened in the fairytales we read. As a matter of fact, I was in my early thirties, preparing my children for their day in our Northern Virginia, suburban home when I had that experience for the first time. Robins. A robin's song seeped into our home from the kitchen window. It was so surreal I stopped mid-stride to identify the foreign sound and investigate its origin. Perched happily on its branch parallel to the window, a robin in a nest I never took note of before bellowed into the morning. Whether it was pride, a sense of accomplishment, or security I couldn't say, but something swept over me knowing I'd achieved a life for my children more similar to that of a fairytale than my urban upbringing.

Sirens, shouts announcing the commencement of a brawl, and gunshots played staccato through our days. A pop in the air always signified someone getting shot or being shot at. In the suburbs, pops were fireworks. Living in a 'good' neighborhood meant you could catch someone feeling comfortable enough to jog outside for exercise. People didn't take leisure jogs around the hood. Anyone jogging or running was either late for something, trying not to miss a bus, or had just done something they needed to distance themselves from.

For the most part, my waking expectations were the same as most around the way. There wasn't a clear path littered with opportunities for me to follow. Each day I had to forge a path, scavenge for opportunities, and negotiate resources. Hustle a dollar, stay alive and one step ahead of anyone else in these streets who thought they could outsmart you, regardless of who they were to you. Friend could become foe in the blink of an eye if it meant a come up in any way. People needed to survive. It's the most basic human instinct: self-preservation.

My city has one of the highest crime rates in the nation, driven by its poverty and unemployment. You learn growing up that it's all good if someone likes you and to have friends, but it's not the most pressing thing in the world. Taking care of yourself and doing what you have to do for you and yours takes precedence. You couldn't count on your buddies all of the time. In the streets, it's either you or them at the end of the day. Sure, you had extremely close bonds and didn't want to cross a friend, but life in the hood gave you very few choices.

I'm from the 17th state to be added to the union. Originally, Ohio was the Buckeye State, named for its unique buckeye trees. Even to this day, our state's football team references our state tree and history. Science and engineering, manufacturing, automotive, metals fabrication, and electronic equipment were the pillars of the economy: blue-collar industries. Meaning, these jobs didn't create much income for the local employees. They were low paying jobs with the exception of a few, and I mean it was an exception. The higher paying positions didn't go to us. Families with one or multiple children had little to go around on such scant income needed to provide shelter, food, clothes, and basic essentials.

It was this social imbalance and economic draught my parents introduced me to at birth. Life is much different when all you have to consider is yourself. Once a small, helpless mouth joins the party, dynamics shift.

University Hospital's Rainbow Babies and Children's Hospital delivered me into a harsh world to face harsher realities in 1988. The facility was one of the city's major historical accomplishments. Established in the late 1860s, the original structure was a single hospital located inside of a two-story home. It was first known as the Wilson Street Hospital. Inspired by the community's dire need for medical attention, local leaders founded it and made do with the limited resources at their disposal. When the operation outgrew its location, it moved to the Marine Hospital building and became Cleveland City Hospital, and later, Lakeside Hospital.

> **THERE WASN'T A CLEAR PATH LITTERED WITH OPPORTUNITIES FOR ME TO FOLLOW.**

In the early 1890s obstetrics and women's services were offered, while Rainbow Cottage provided care to sick children. The medical system continued to extend its services. John Macleod's academic work leading to the discovery of insulin was done here. Charles Hoover was credited with establishing Hoover's sign here. The growing system instituted the first school of nurse anesthesia. This proud organization can proudly boast being the birthing place of many more great medical discoveries and inventions. It eventually formed the region's first multihospital system and joined the University Hospitals. Many considered it to be a big deal to land a job at the facility. Sadly enough, the original structure isn't there anymore. It was torn down years ago since no one cared to maintain the site. I felt the city should have preserved all of that history as a historical landmark where they could have offered tours and education. But no; nothing remains.

That's one of the saddest things to me. We demolish so many sentimental, nostalgic, historical landmarks, significant and less, in the name of moving communities forward. We tend to underestimate the value and importance of maintaining connections to the past forerunners and their achievements. When we don't see what we accomplished around us, we forget our progress and fail

> **MY CITY HAS ONE OF THE HIGHEST CRIME RATES IN THE NATION, DRIVEN BY ITS POVERTY AND UNEMPLOYMENT.**

to progress. We have a difficult time accepting our potential and believing in our worth. We are robbed of evidence of our contributions to communities and cities, states and nations others claim as fruits of their labor.

So here I was, a brown beauty born to a 23-year-old mother who, with and due to my father, was addicted to drugs. The pair was such a mess my father's name never made it to the birth certificate. He was physically present, but who knows what was going on with him mentally for him to not sign his own child's birth certificate. The conditions under which I was born seemed as if life tried to designate me as the beneficiary of generational dysfunction.

My mother made it to the age of maturity before she met the big time drug dealer ten years her senior. Young and naïve, she plunged head over hills for him. Though their relationship was new, family and friends had known about him since he was young. Michael Eaton, better known as Herc, did stints in boy's homes since he was 12-years-old and divorced the education system after 8th grade. He was unruly and no one in the family was willing to take him in. Everyone had their own issues, their own bad kids, bills, mouths to feed, and clothes to buy. A hard-headed, street-bound adolescent was a hard sell. It would also mean they had to run around tracking him down. No one had a spare second in the day for such foolishness.

As if that wasn't enough, he argued with adults and was quick to fight the male members of his family. Herc had never hit a female family member but it didn't seem beyond him. Positive male influence was lost on him unless he invited it: which he didn't. The male mentors he picked up were more criminal and ruthless than he. His mother didn't have the energy to chase him in the streets and she got tired of trying to get him to attend school. She was the only one who cared enough to even try.

"I can't make money in school so there's no reason for me to be there." He would rationalize.

After a few intense conversations with the school system regarding his bouts of absence and his refusal to stay out of the streets and in class, he was placed in a boy's home. Keep in mind, when he neglected school he ran the streets. He didn't sit home to watch television and eat cereal. So not only was he not being formally educated, he was racking up deviant traits and activities.

From what I could tell whenever he spoke about his experiences, it didn't seem as if he cared or felt remorse for his behavior. He was around other inner-city miscreants in the boy's home, sharing tricks of the trades and forming bad habits. The streets had won. It had lured another black youth with its siren song of fast cash, good times, and freedom. He was so busy having fun and making change he didn't notice he was being swallowed whole.

I'm baffled at how intelligent he became, in spite of. People don't realize how much more knowledge you obtain on the streets than in a class setting. Life is the greatest teacher. Books and lectures, workbooks and homework are theoretic-black and white, true or false. Even critical thinking courses don't teach you about the real world and its many layers and players. It isn't honest about the true bad guys, their agendas, and the game stacked against you. You get the real deal when life is your sensei, not the approved version edited to support social constructs and agendas. But like far too many of our black men, he applied his talents to the wrong endeavors.

My mother's upbringing was a bit different. Her aunt Regina was 18-years-old when she purchased the house on the east side at the corner of Elberon and E. 125th for her mother, my great-grandma, Alice Ruth Hutchins. Aunt Genie, as we call her, started a great career with the phone company straight out of high school. The company actually wanted her to begin working the day after she graduated, but she wanted a slight break first and negotiated her start date two weeks after. Black people at that time, and especially in Cleveland, weren't capturing opportunities like that often. They were like unicorns. We definitely didn't have, or know we had, negotiating power. Yet, aunt Genie's intellect was apparent and she was well spoken so her interview impressed the company in comparison to enough of her competitors that she made the cut.

What also helped was the time she spent at John Hay Business School mastering secretarial skills. I can count on one hand how many of us could type, navigate computer programs and operate office equipment. I overheard her frequently speaking about how the other blacks in the office she worked at, all janitors, looked at her like she was alien and uppity. She was the only person of color not pushing a mop. Most of the people in our community worked hotel hospitality, transportation, call centers, security, education, or labor. This was her life for thirty-five years until she retired. Another bragging point we constantly endured.

She refused to allow herself to be associated with anyone who held themselves to a lower standard than she did. Aunt Genie thought very highly of herself, which was reflected in the company she kept. Even as a teenager she never formed intimate relationships with troubled, inner-city peers. If you weren't doing something with your life she had nothing for you.

Aunt Genie's upbringing made her ford tough. The only girl in a house with three brothers, she was raised to believe the same rules didn't apply to her as they did to them. No one ever questioned the fairness of it. It was what it was.

"Girls can't do what boys can." My grandma would declare. "It's just the way things are. Boys are always going to get in trouble. They do crazy mess all the time and they don't think things through. Girls are smarter." As if that was consolation for the double standard. "You don't have time to get mixed up in mess and get in trouble. Keep your head straight and in those books."

My aunt and uncle's lives are direct results of this belief system. My uncles got away with murder and all anyone heard from my grandma was, "Boys will be boys." Meanwhile, aunt Genie's life was constantly under a microscope and all of her actions or decisions were heavily scrutinized.

Thankfully, aunt Genie was no fool. She worked hard, she kept clear of wayward activities and bad crowds, and focused on making something out of her life. Aunt Genie didn't forget where she came from or who made her into who she became. The first thing she did was stack her paychecks. My granddad drove her to work for the first six months because she didn't have a car. As soon as she had enough, she brought one. Brand new. If she was going to pay for something it would be exactly what she wanted. Her taste was high end from the beginning. She didn't want anything previously owned. I'm very much like her in that way. We love independence, being able to do for ourselves, and having the best.

The next thing aunt Genie did was save seventeen thousand dollars to purchase my grandma's house. They say she wept when aunt Genie handed her the keys and the deed. The gift's exterior was yellow and white with wide gray steps leading you up to the porch. It wasn't the largest home, but we made do with the three bedrooms and one bathroom. The house actually had an additional half bathroom but it was in the unfinished basement so no one used it.

This was how my mom was brought up. In a family owned home. She was surrounded by relatives who valued work ethic, generational wealth building, and support. Strong women who laid out the framework for being such. Whenever she hit a wall, she had people ready to help catapult her over it. We didn't give up on ours. If help was needed, help was offered. My mom grew up without a want or a care.

Our family was akin to The Jeffersons on the block. Our kind didn't own homes. We overpaid slum lords to reside in older, unkept, and often dilapidated structures. And while the rent may have been lower than better neighborhoods, it didn't mean we deserved living conditions less humane. We enriched the property owners while sinking further and further into an impoverished state.

Home ownership was a far-fetched dream in our community; leaving property to hand down from generation to generation. It was also impractical to many because we weren't educated in managing resources, prioritizing responsibilities, and valuing assets. Instead of passing it down as an inheritance, the few people we did know who owned homes either lost them to the bank, sold them for quick cash they blew, or eventually took chump change as compensation to clear their land for new developments.

Investors came in all the time to buy up properties to rent or flip in rural communities. They realized it was more cost efficient to clear land here to build than the older structures in more affluent areas. This practice interested me so much I reviewed the process. It started making sense why there were so many abandoned properties, or as we called them, bandos. So instead of investors coming in and improving value in the city, we were left with monstrous eyesores containing corpses from criminal activities, emptied vials of drugs, shattered glass, and litter.

Few of us understood home ownership as wealth or a potential source of income as landlords. Mortgage was only a bill, a burden. Wealth, for those who were less financially educated, was straight up cash and measured in the quantity of material items possessed like shoes, clothes, cars, and jewelry. So, for a family to have made the decision to purchase a home instead of making frivolous transactions, they were wise, different…on a whole other level.

My family lived on Elberon for thirty-seven years. I was the only child, growing up among my great uncle Terry, my cousin Greg a.k.a Jaimel, great-grandmother Alice who everyone called Ruth, and great-granddad Buster. I referred to Jamiel as my uncle since he was eighteen years older than me, but in reality, he was my second cousin. Life is different for a child growing up with elders; the dynamics in the house, the music, the rules, and the food.

No, the house didn't smell like mothballs and I did have a life, but there was more order than I witnessed when I visited homes with multiple children or young parents. I also probably ate better at home than most of them. Their houses were full of sugar-filled, processed foods. The only vegetables or fruits they consumed were out of cans or jars. The only time they saw collards being cleaned, green beans getting snapped, or corn shucked was during the holidays.

My great-grandma, who I called grandma because great-grandma was a lot and no one else was competing for the title in my daily life, loved to make salmon croquettes with grits, scrambled eggs with cheese, and biscuits. Now that was real food. She didn't believe in feeding her family junk. Everything she cooked was from scratch. Watching her in the kitchen whipping up her magic, I learned measurements took the heart out of the dish. Her eyes were her tablespoons and cups. Her cooking also taught me packaged food had nothing on the flavoring of proper home cooked meals.

I'd see her put ingredients in a meal your taste buds would never identify. She'd tell me it was to cut the bite of another ingredient, to bolster the flavor, or act as a binding agent. There was always something to distinguish it as her own version. I'd shadow her around the kitchen, making inquiries and taste testing. What kid doesn't love sampling food while it's cooking? Just like any other, my favorite was licking the whisk after cake batter was prepped.

When I think back over all of the support and love that got me where I am and through my storms, it was her. Even after her death, it was her. Quality time was never in short supply. Sure, who I am was embedded in my DNA, but my confidence, sense of family, and accountability came from her. She was the most supportive person in my life. She fed my spirit. If I fell short, building me up was the only option, not cutting me down. Anything I conjured up to endeavor, she rooted me on. Nothing was beyond my potential.

"If you want something, what's to stop you but you baby?" She would ask rhetorically. When I wasn't putting my best effort into something, or I was jeopardizing a goal, she would hit me with her favorite line, "I got mines, you betta get yours." Out of her four children, two grandchildren and one great grand; she, myself, aunt Genie, and my mom were the only ones to earn their diplomas. I can still hear her saying this to me whenever I'm messing up. The statement's purpose was to encourage us to do our best. "I got mines, you betta get yours."

This was our expression of love: support. We were people of action, not words. If something was real we needed to see it, not hear about it. Needless to say, there was not a bunch of lovey-dovey banter crowding the air of our home. You knew you were loved and secure. No one constantly reaffirmed your feelings. No softies came from Ruth's tribe. It actually would be on the other end of a collect call from jail before I heard the heart-melting "I love you" drip like sweet honey out of Ruth's mouth. But that's a story for another day.

WEST COAST SHORTY

The earliest part of my life I can discuss from my own memory is Vegas. My mother moved there when I was an infant to reunite with my father in the hopes of building a solid foundation for me by having both parents in the home. The only time my father wasn't in the streets doing drugs was when he was incarcerated for selling them. His rap sheet included other offenses like robbery, grand larceny, and the most horrifying of them all- especially for a daughter to find out, rape. Rape. Let that sink in. This man, my father, the man who taught me to defend myself and loved me, raped a woman. The man who would have taken the life of any other male who violated me in this way did that very unforgivable thing to another woman. Trust and believe I inquired about the circumstances surrounding the allegations on multiple occasions. No clarification was ever offered. It angered me for a while. I couldn't look at or speak with him. Who was this man who fathered me? If he could do this, what else was he capable of? What else did I not know about him? It was a lot for me to digest. I had so many questions that needed answers I knew I would never get.

So while he was incarcerated for the majority of our sin city residency, he was close enough for us to visit. Regardless of their relationship, my mother was always there for him. He had her smuggling narcotics inside for him during her visits. I found this to be super dumb when I was old enough to hear about it because she risked being caught and locked up herself, leaving her child to be cared for by family if the state didn't take me. I guess that's why he married her. She was his ride or die at the expense of my or her own well-being.

> **HIS RAP SHEET INCLUDED OTHER OFFENSES LIKE ROBBERY, GRAND LARCENY, AND THE MOST HORRIFYING OF THEM ALL- ESPECIALLY FOR A DAUGHTER TO FIND OUT, RAPE. RAPE. LET THAT SINK IN. THIS MAN, MY FATHER, THE MAN WHO TAUGHT ME TO DEFEND MYSELF AND LOVED ME, RAPED A WOMAN.**

I'll never fully understand their relationship. I get love is a beast all its own. I know every union is unique, but when the foundation is compromised and the chemistry is poison, you question the health of it. Strangely enough, I couldn't tell who meant more to whom. I always thought my mom loved him more because of all she did for him and how she followed him even though he was incarcerated. But in retrospect, my mom was the only woman he married, despite having children with other women, including the mother of his current 6-year-old daughter while being in his 60's. That says a lot. Men don't jump into marriage and offer their names frivolously. They'll lay up with you all day, playing house and making empty promises. Marriage, the full monty, was for a woman you couldn't live without. They didn't come a dime a dozen. Men don't fall in love every day.

It was during these tender, formative years that I was introduced to bullying in such a traumatizing manner the memories are with me to this day. I guess I wasn't much different from most children that age in terms of the early constructs of social development and behavior. The difference is how prepared I was to deal with it being an only child. Siblings tend to tease and harass each other. When you are raised in a home with other children, you become accustomed to sharing toys and the fights which ensue when no one wants to share them. You fight for attention and learn to co-exist. Only children who are not heavily socialized are often deprived of this lesson.

There tend to always be aggressive children who haven't been disciplined enough to not assert their wills on others. Then you have the spoiled brats who can't come to terms with not getting what they want so they simply take it. The other character is the one who pushes the limits until they find the boundary, then try to push it back further.

As an only child, no conflict of interest or attack on my happiness ever presented itself. I was loved and I had my mother's attention when she was home. All of my toys were at my disposable and there was no one for me to quarrel with over anything.

It's interesting, what makes one a bully. I've learned many children develop the horrible character trait as a defense mechanism from being bullied themselves. It happened to be the case with me. While my being bullied turned me into a proponent for anti-bullying, the resolve to protect myself transformed me into what I disliked. This reality only struck me once I started reminiscing over the events of my life to write this book. Eventually, I determined I was tougher than the bullies so I would bully the bullies to assert my dominance; and if I noticed they were harassing someone who couldn't stand up for themselves, I would step in as their defender.

Our home in Vegas was an apartment complex but it resembled an old fashioned motel with brick stairs bordered by railings on both sides that wound up to the next floor and had a metal pole going up the center of the stairway. The apartments encircled an open courtyard. We weren't in the most affluent section of town if you haven't guessed. There were no drug raids or prostitution rings being run out of it, but it resembled all of the motels you saw in those types of seedy movies, just a bit cleaner.

Well, across the compound in the apartments facing ours lived a white little boy and his power wheel. This boy would purposefully, and frequently, haul his car down the stairs, get on it, ride it over to my side, bite me, and return to the sanctuary of his apartment. Literally. The events surrounding when and how it started or when and how it ended are hazy, but those moments remain vivid. I'm also not sure why I stood there and allowed him to get close enough to repeat the act after the first few times. Surely I had to catch on to his intentions and know what I was in store for once it occurred two or three times. He never offered me a ride on his power wheel or tried to play so… A nip of my skin was all he had interest in.

Then there was a white little girl downstairs from me who formed the irritating habit of throwing dirt in my hair. I don't remember her doing this to anyone else. But when she saw me, she immediately felt my scalp needed dirt on it. I tried avoiding her because my mom would ask why I had so much dirt in my hair after playing outside. Knowing black mothers, dirt in hair equaled having to get the dirt out before you got in your bed, which translated into doing your hair which ultimately ended in more work for them. On a consistent basis, it became not only an issue for me, but an issue for my mom. This crossed her off the list of children I cared to play with; leaving two black sisters in the apartments across the complex.

Playing with the sisters would have been ideal except for their affinity for horrifying me with stories about the boogeyman and monsters. They even went so far as to place warning signs on their doors saying monsters were inside. It seemed like a period of torment for me. All children were bad company and the only one I could expect to have fun with, safely and happily, was myself. No wonder when I returned to Cleveland those experiences shaped me and prepared me for what I was to endure in the inner city.

HOME SWEET HOME

Most families have a Big Ma or whatever name they give the matriarch of their family. *Soul Food* was a primary depiction of her role. Matriarch's hold families together, keep the order, pass down the history and traditions, nurture, provide emotional and spiritual support, defend, reprimand, and are a fountain of love. Families are stable and happy while the matriarchs are with them. They are like water to the roots of a tree: thirst quenching and refreshing. Whether you were directly raised by her or not she was instrumental in your care and upbringing.

My mother's father's grandmother raised my mother until she passed away, then his mother took care of my mother. This same woman assumed responsibility for me when she got tired of my mother traipsing me in and out of crack houses or any other unsavory crevice of East Cleveland. Several conversations were had about my safety and quality of care. Enough was clearly enough. The idea was not to strip my mother of her role as such. She had been given ample opportunities to prioritize her life and make the best choices for me and giving me to my father was not a viable option.

My parents didn't have it together enough to appreciate the joys and rewards of parenthood. They couldn't divorce the poisons ruling their desires or manage themselves well enough to raise me. Denise Jackson and Michael Eaton, a.k.a Deedee and Herc, relinquished that delight to Alice Ruth Hutchins, my mother's father's mother. It seemed every time they even thought of breaking free, the addiction sent it's minions to rope them in. Friends over here, parties over there, stress everywhere. Addiction met them on every corner, in conversations, invaded dreams. And although it robbed them of precious moments and experiences with their child, it took much more than that. It stole and buried pieces of them. Some they never even noticed were missing because they lost them before they were even aware of their existence. Untapped potentials and unknown opportunities, lost.

It appeared my parents found it easier to let go of their children than their habits. I say 'children' because while I was my mother's first, my father had three daughters before me, each scattered around Cleveland being raised by their single mothers. If you find my family dynamic stressed or untraditional, what you have to understand is this was our norm. 'Our,' meaning the 80's babies of urban America. Grandparents became parents by proxy while their children were swept up by the cocaine and crack craze of the '70s and '80s. So when I looked around and saw the majority of my friends and other family members were being raised by grandparents and aunts as myself, the plight escaped me. Thank God for the villages which were in place to raise the children or we would have been lost.

This, however, caused issues with parenting in the following generations. The model set was birth parents leaving their offspring in the custody of grandparents and gallivanting off to enjoy their lives, checking in on occasion. Traditional, two-parent households became blessings and oddities instead of the norm, while the effects of these untraditional family systems were very real and apparent in the behavior and psyche of those living it.

Youth believed they could have children and pass them off to a family member while they continued on in similar fashion as their parents. Papas were no longer the only rolling stones. Mothers were doing their own thing too. If they realized a bit too late their assumed safety net wouldn't catch their fall, abortion or adoption became a mother's next moves. It was the age of babies having babies since there was no accountability and responsibility.

The sad thing is many of us joked about our relationships with our parents. We would tell each other if we saw their mother or father around town. The child would joke about us seeing their parents more than they did and how long it had been since they saw them. Feelings of insecurity or inadequacy plagued many of us due to this. *Do I deserve love if my parents didn't find me valuable enough to stick around and provide it? Was I a mistake? Am I a burden to the family who took me in?*

As a mother now, I couldn't imagine this. Not waking to my children, being their counsel, comfort and protection, ensuring they ate and putting them in bed at night, knowing their whereabouts on a daily basis. How it would impact my children if I abandoned them. It would take death for me to give this away. Although I acknowledge there are many parents whose situation didn't offer them a chance, I'm thankful for mine. Separation from my children isn't an option.

> **IT APPEARED MY PARENTS FOUND IT EASIER TO LET GO OF THEIR CHILDREN THAN THEIR HABITS.**

Years of living and interacting with my mother provided revelation into her struggle. She hadn't so much offered me up as a willing sacrifice to other family members. Her addiction had such a strong hold on her she couldn't keep a hold on me. It threw her life into convulsive patterns, surrendering to the wind all in her possession, including me. Ruth talked DeeDee into allowing her to save me from herself. Had she not, I would have been weathering the storms with her like my younger sister Diamond, but we'll get to that later.

I never even questioned if Deedee was an unfit parent. I was young, innocent, and happy enough with my grandma I didn't consider an alternative. She was strict but I loved being with her. I needed the discipline and structure she offered. My mouth and attitude were a recipe for disaster. Left unchecked, I could have easily been killed in the streets or incarcerated. Had I been raised under the negligence of my parents, things could have gone much worse.

Deedee was the one who struggled visibly with the arrangement. She wanted the ultimate say in my rearing without being the main caregiver. I knew this always bothered her but I didn't care. You gotta pay the cost to be the boss, and my grandma was the one paying, not her. I can remember a day she came to see me and witnessed my grandma feeding me pork. She verbalized her disapproval. A juicy piece of pig never bothered me. I loved a chop, slice of bacon, rack of rib…you name it. Pork, in her opinion, was an unclean meat and not fit for consumption. My grandma asked her to consider whether pork was more detrimental than what she consumed. Pork or crack, which is more harmful?

Another thing I learned from her. She didn't back down for anyone so you better had come correct when you stepped to her. There was no need in addressing anything she did if your life wasn't together. You know the bible verse, *Take the plank out of your own eye before trying to remove the speck from your brothers*. Oh, she definitely applied that to people approaching her.

My mother's issue with pork was a conundrum to me. She and my dad refused to eat it. This was something they had unwavering intolerance about. They lacked the fortitude to refrain from using and abusing drugs and alcohol for the majority of their lives, but pork! Swine! God forbid. Well, actually he did. But their position was still a bit hypocritical.

A crack house on Lakeview Ave. was one of my mom's favorite hangout spots. It didn't have the obvious appearance of the events taking place within its walls, but everyone knew what went down there. I, unlike some of my peers, knew where to find my parents if I really want to, which I seldom did. I don't recall going there to find her, but I remember a child, Demetrius, lived in the house amongst all the debauchery. He wasn't fortunate to have someone rescue him from it. That was his village. He saw dope fiends nodding off first hand in his home. The place he ate and slept was overrun by addicts and bums.

People strolled in and out all hours of the day or night. It had to be a rough upbringing. Every now and again a fight erupted over an accusation of stolen product, money, or items missing from the house. I can't imagine how that must have been for him, but I assume he found a way to cope. It would've been hard for me to feel comfortable living in that environment. The idea of my property being stolen was intolerable. And on top of that, to support a drug addiction! Nah. I'm grateful I was spared that life.

Obviously, God clearly had plans and angels on assignment over him. He didn't become a product of his environment. Last I heard he overcame all of the obstacles his upbringing presented and went on to become a boxer. Nothing big. Local events here and there; helping train the youth in the community. Demetrius and I weren't in the same circles for me to witness how he grew into the role, but I'm glad anytime I hear even one of us survived.

By surviving, I'm not just talking walking and breathing. Surviving means avoiding being taken under by our city and what the streets offered. It means becoming a productive member of society and not a drain or shame to the community. Surviving means being in a position to reach back, and down, to pull another up so they too may defeat the odds. This doesn't discredit those of us who went through subjugation, but fought our way out. Those of us are even more victorious because the fight is much harder when you succumb and have to claw your way out versus never having experienced the struggle at all. Take it from me, I know. My journey to where I am wasn't a squeaky clean one.

Not having my mother in my life in the traditional sense probably did affect me deeper than I knew. I tried very hard not to dwell on it. When I thought of my mother, during my young and naïve years, and how she chose to live her life, I wondered why she couldn't just get it together. Then again, could I have expected her to grasp the importance of overcoming in order to nurture and raise her own child if her mother didn't do it for her? She had been raised lovingly by her grandmother, but lacked an example of a birth mother/daughter relationship. To nurture and care for what came from your own body, to identify genetic features and patterns of behavior.

It is easy to the absence of her mother would have ignited a passion, born of pain and empathy, to be there for her child. Did she not long for her own mother? Wonder about the cause of her absence? Was there no bitterness in her as a result of her mother's choice to abandon her? Were there no painful memories of children with their birth parents and the feelings of envy they created? Guess not enough to count.

> **NOT HAVING MY MOTHER IN MY LIFE IN THE TRADITIONAL SENSE PROBABLY DID AFFECT ME DEEPER THAN I KNEW.**

In addition, everyone doesn't deal with trauma in the same manner. She put in the effort to be a mother to me for a short while after my birth, but the physical and emotional abuse from my father took its toll. The euphoria of having me was overshadowed by the affliction she endured at the hands of the love of her life. The very same drugs he introduced to her became the coping tools she used to deal with the life he led her into. So, I guess I also blamed my father for preventing my mother from being available for me. It still didn't give her a free pass. I just wish she fought her demons harder. I wish having me gave her the extra push she needed to go on when she felt weak, or lost, or defeated.

My mother's mother, Connie, was a prostitute. Clearly, she found herself in a situation where this was the better of all evils offering sufficient income. I sit back now and laugh at the generational curses that tried to bind themselves to me. Life always comes full circle unless someone breaks the cycle, but we'll put a pin in that for now.

All seven of Connie's children had been placed in foster care because of her profession. It's sad when I think about it. A large portion of my family wasn't raised by their biological parents. Her children's situation was more dire than mine though so I won't even act as if I could relate. See, the 'system' isn't often the optimal environment to grow up in. Many children suffer exposure to so many things they should never encounter at their ages and it gives them a disposition to unfavorable behavior.

Luckily, although my grandmother was a prostitute, she knew the identity of my mother's father. Ruth acknowledged the child despite the circumstances of her conception. Her son got a prostitute pregnant, but she harbored no feelings for her. The child was blood. Ruth knew from early on Connie wouldn't be able to keep the child. She hadn't kept the ones before her. While Ruth never doubted Connie had love for her children as a mother, she knew she lacked the ability to raise them. She, unlike her siblings, would escape the system.

Even revisiting this truth gives me more compassion for my mother. How must it be to have a mother engaging in prostitution? Being the product of a cheap, filthy transaction. I wonder if my mother considered herself a disgrace to her father, though it was of no fault of her own? Immature, irresponsible parents tend to blame their children for their mishaps when they have a hard time facing themselves in the mirror. She couldn't have felt complete. Knowing I have an entire branch of family I know nothing about opens a void within me, and I'm generations removed. It took her a while to even locate her siblings. She went years without knowing anything about them. How must that have been? To not know if your siblings are healthy or safe or happy? Then what about the guilt of being the one to got to stay with family? Not all of their father's families were known or came to the rescue. I'll never be able to thank my grandma enough for stepping in to meet my need.

ELBERON

Tamira lived in the dirtiest house on my grandma's block. I mean trifling. This was the type of house you got roasted for if people found out you lived there, and they did. They got joked so much it didn't bother them after a point. The basement was always flooded which caused a putrid smell. You couldn't miss it. Even if you didn't come onto the property and just walked by you got smacked in the nostrils. No amount of potpourri or fragrance plug-ins could have masked that stench. We traced the odor once and peeped in out of curiosity after wondering where the stench was coming from. To be honest, I thought they had stale food in the fridge or rotten trash stashed somewhere. I even considered the possibility of dead rodents or something because I had never seen a flooded basement before.

"Ew!" A little girl from the neighborhood complained. "Your house is funky!"

"Our house don't stink!" Tamira shot back in defense. "It's just our basement sometimes."

"What's wrong with your basement?" I asked. Our basement was unfinished but it never produced this horrid odor.

"We don't know! Our momma just tells us to stay from down there. We don't have the money to get it fixed." Her brother Deonte jumped in. "Wanna see?" He ran toward the door and flung it open.

We were immediately assaulted by a waft of nauseating fumes. But, kids being kids, we sauntered right over and crowded together in the door frame, peering down into the dimly lit corridor. It smelled like things were dead and rotting down there. A shallow pool of greenish brown water sat stagnantly. Out of nowhere, I felt myself being shoved forward.

"Hey!" I turned around to face the prankster. Mario, her other brother, called himself trying to scare me. I shoved him away from me and distanced myself from the doorway.

"Mario you always playing too much!" Tamira barked at him.

I learned the children with the worst kept houses had the most freedom and fun because their parents obviously didn't care for the most part. Their mother laid in her room all day with trash littering the floors and overflowing the trashcans. The only time she ever left her haven was for her security job at the airport. I don't even know how she kept the job with her funky self. She wore the same soiled uniform each shift.

When she was holed up in her room, the only company she kept was the hundreds of emptied Dr. Pepper cans and bottles, discarded on the floor. The beverage was a main staple of her daily diet. She qualified for her own episode on Hoarders. The floors were so dirty we never knew the original color. A black film covered it, making it nasty and sticky. You hated going inside but it's where we had the most fun; especially during the winter when no one wanted to deal with the cold blitzing through the city from Lake Erie. Had my grandma known I was in that pigsty she would have had a conniption and scrubbed the black off me, not trusting an inch to have escaped contamination.

Tamira's two brothers, Deonte and Mario, were bad as hell. Deonte more so. I had the horrible misfortune of seeing him beat a baby bird, separated from its nest, to death in his backyard with a wooden stick riddled with rusty nails. Being an animal lover, I believed there was something to say about the depth of cruelty within a person who could hurt helpless animals. And he wasn't doing it out of curiosity, or defense. He wasn't playing too rough with it by misjudging his strength. He genuinely liked it. There was a smile on his face and satisfaction curling the corners of his mouth in response to the pain he inflicted on this poor baby bird. It died after only a few moments from its wounds. When he realized there was no more fun to have tormenting the thing, he moved on to find another source of entertainment. The baby bird's corpse remained under the tree its family still inhabited.

The Conley kids-They didn't have a father figure in the home. Many of us didn't. Yet, it seemed this affected them in the worse possible way. Deonte had a tendency to feel girls up and take it as far as he could. I don't recall him ever being successful enough to penetrate anyone, but I doubt that was from lack of trying. He was super mannish and it was such dangerous behavior which could and may have led to deeper trauma for some. I was in the clear because I didn't let it get that far. I won't lie, he got his fair share of feels off of me too. He was four years older than us so he definitely knew what he was doing. We considered it normal and never snitched since we saw it happening to one another and no one else was telling. At least you were cute enough for someone to want to touch you, right? The reasoning of young girls is like that. It would have messed with our self-esteem had he never tried and we noticed him pursuing others. That may, in fact, have actually triggered us to initiate the act. Even if we weren't thinking about him, had we caught a glimpse of him giving another girl attention, we would have spent a second or two comparing ourselves to discern why it wasn't us. The funny thing is, we didn't even like him like that. The issue was our own validation.

The first time I remember being touched by him we were playing on their nasty couch. The couch was so dirty clouds of dust flew up when you plopped down on it. We played on it anyway. He straight up felt on my 'girl parts' as if it was nothing and no one was around, except it was something and we weren't alone. The feeling was foreign for me at 7-years-old, but the sensation admittedly piqued my curiosity. He continued his pass and grabs from time to time but he never lingered. Part of me now wonders if he had been doing it so long that he just started unconsciously touching familiar girls in passing. Wouldn't have surprised me. It got to the point if one of us saw him coming we would just step out of his reach. If he kept trying we would deal with it. If he kept it moving, he kept it moving.

> **THE FIRST TIME I REMEMBER BEING TOUCHED BY HIM WE WERE PLAYING ON THEIR NASTY COUCH.**

After all that groping and fondling, Deonte turned to guys. Isn't that the way? I never saw him attempt physical contact with a boy when we were young and I don't know what caused the switch. Maybe it was always there. He wasn't flamboyant, at first, so we didn't know of any other signs to consider. I think back to when he began dying his hair various colors midway through high school. Was that when it started? Sisqo was hot at the time so guys were getting away with it, kinda. Nothing made us suspicious.

Still, his looks always matched his house: dirty. His skin had the appearance of being in constant need of cleaning. It seemed as if it had a dinginess to it which refused to be washed away. The dyed hair didn't do the intended job of making him more attractive. A lot of the colors were actually a bit much on him. We just chalked it up to him going through a phase and switching up his style. Hell, most of us did at that age. Dying your hair was a cheap cosmetic change. You could go right to a beauty supply store or drug store, get a box, and do it at home yourself.

Tamira and her brothers weren't particularly popular. You knew them or you didn't and it mattered not either way. They were in the background, like so many, meandering from day to day. But they weren't heavy into anything. That's why Deonte's untimely death was so unfortunate. I don't know what led to it, but he was found murdered on Martin Luther King Blvd. Many in the community believed it was a hate crime. He was only nineteen or twenty, but that was Cleveland.

Their brother, Mario, became affiliated with the gang named 'Folks'. Gangs were a way of life for us. You could say they were our Skull and Bones. You idolized them when you were growing up and either chose the one you wanted or it chose you. And like so many others who refused to sweat and bleed for pennies and crappy benefits, he turned to serving street pharmaceuticals for the locals.

But back to Tamira. When I first returned to Cleveland I was a loner. I didn't have any friends so I rode my bike up and down the street by myself. I was fine with that. To be honest, I was accustomed to it. Tamira took note of this and decided to try me. If she was inside and saw me outside, she came out. She started pushing me off my bike. Try as I may, I couldn't avoid her. I was prohibited from going any further than our block by myself and her house was four down from mine. I was still developing into my 'don't take shit from anybody' self, but I hadn't arrived there yet. I would just get back on my bike and keep it moving. She would walk along the sidewalk as I pedaled, then run up on me and assault me. Minor cuts and scrapes started adding up on my arms and legs from the impact with the street. I'd try to pedal away or tell her to leave me alone, but it seemed I was the most entertaining part of her day.

Until this one day, my father was outside and saw it. He had been perched on the hood of a car speaking to the father of a set of twins who lived at the top of our block. Every time they saw each other they stopped what they were doing and gravitated toward each other. Mostly they spoke sports and what was going on with people they knew from the streets. They could be spotted talking outside often since my parents lived in the duplex on the other side of my grandma's house after we returned from Vegas. Needless to say, being that close to my grandma, I spent a night or two with my parents but opted to reside with her. This worked out for all parties involved because although my parents were present they weren't involved.

Anyway, my father watched Tamira knock me off my bike about four times before he hopped off the hood of the car and leisurely strolled down the street in our direction. He called me to meet him on the porch of our house.

"You gonna take that motherfucking bike in the house, then you gonna go back down the street and whip her ass." He hissed between clenched teeth. There was no room for consideration in his voice. That was what was going to happen whether I was ready for it or not. He ended it with the typical statement of parents who are hell-bent on training their children to defend and protect themselves, "If you don't whip her ass I'll whip yo' ass and you won't come back outside for the rest of the summer."

Not every child born in the hood started out as a fighter. It was the parents who knew the hood would chew you up and not even bother to spit you out who cultivated whatever self-defense mechanisms they found in you. My father knew I was scared. What he was trying to prevent was me being afraid to address conflict, physical or otherwise, for the rest of my life.

There I was, in my pink, plastic teddy bear glasses on the brink of turning a major page in my life. I slowly hoisted the bike up the stairs and retired it for the day, along with my beloved pink frames and a piece of my innocence, then returned back outside, shaking with adrenaline. Knowing if he hadn't stayed by my side the entire time I would have aborted the mission, he escorted me down the block to her front steps where her brothers and their friend were sitting. It's weird, but each time the memory of this day resurfaces, I always recall the huge log on the porch first.

"Where's your sister?" My father demanded.

"She's in the house. Why?" Mario responded. The boys looked at each other with overconfident glances and turned back to us. There was minor posturing to communicate they were in charge since we were on their property.

"'Cause they about to fight." My father declared. The group of young street punks were of no consequence to him. There was a lesson to be had in this for his daughter; one he was determined she learn today. He knew how things were at their age. He ran with fools like them once upon a time. Most young people were just bark, but every once in a while you ran into quite a bite. These boys weren't going to be much of an obstacle.

"You ain't about to fight me." Tamira said, appearing on the porch. More bark. No worries. Perhaps Tamira needed to learn something today too.

"Oh, she is definitely about to fight you today." My father corrected her. His stance never changed. His feet were firmly planted hip-width apart. His hands hung loosely by his sides.

Tamira's brothers were situated on either side of the steps and goaded her to pick up the log. Clearly, this was my first rodeo. My father was by my side. They witnessed her harass me countless times before. Yet they still felt it necessary to provoke their sister to fight dirty.

> NOT EVERY CHILD BORN IN THE HOOD STARTED OUT AS A FIGHTER.

My father warned them if she hit me with the log he would be tearing into both of them, period. They didn't press it any further because they realized he wasn't there for games. The three amigos fell back to watch the rest of the events unfold.

Tamira, irritated at the fact she was being forced into combat she didn't initiate, descended the five stairs and stopped in the middle of the walkway leading to the sidewalk. It was long compared to the others on the block. Or maybe it just seemed longer as I watched my opponent approach me when I preferred she didn't. We stood on opposing sides and my father instructed us to begin fighting like a referee. How do you start fighting? How do you kickstart the physical altercation when seconds prior both girls were simply standing, facing each other. The girl wasn't much bigger than me in girth and about my same height, though she was a year younger. She had the same dirty skin her brother had. It was the truest brown, not light or dark. Brown, brown. Everything else about her was nondescript.

I remember it like yesterday. I was so fucking scared as I walked up to her, thinking about how painful it was about to be to get beat up. I hadn't done this before. So I put all my force into propelling my arm toward her and slapped the shit out of her. To my surprise, she didn't even fight back. I learned a very valuable lesson that day: many people will be all talk, and talk is cheap.

Tamira started yelling and screaming, then fled into her house. Going forward, we fought on sight. She had a cousin named Tanay who would attempt to bully me for her. The fear of pain stayed with me when I was faced with a fight, but there was no backing down. Eventually, Tamira and I became friends. It was as if all the scrapping was an initiation process for us. We were both scared of each other. It took years of fist fights, hair pulling, and ground rolling for us to throw off our apprehensions about it each other and let our guards down. This was the story of Tamira and me.

It's also a major introduction to me. For the greater part of my life, I was known as a fighter. Where I'm from, that's the only way you fixed a problem. There was no mediation. No one said, "Come sit with me. Let's talk this thing out." That right there would get you tagged as weak and targeted. Trust me, the very last thing you wanted was to be a target.

Conflict resolution was fist to face, foot to gut. My motto soon became, 'Point them out, I knock them out.' Those were the words you were going to hear if you came to me with drama. If I saw someone who called themselves beefing with me, it was a go on sight. This frame of mind perpetuated stereotypes. It's why we are deemed violent. Our instincts are to fight, not think things through or walk away. That's why we are barred from elite social circles unless we prove ourselves by disowning our culture. Unfortunately, we couldn't be taught better because the ones raising us didn't know better.

What I hoped for in a fight was that the person would be at arm's length. I let them get close. If my fist could reach you, you were catching a fade, and if you got up, all bets were off. Conversations before fights were a no go as well. That was a dummy move. You never gave the opposition a jump on you. This was a fight, not a debate. If someone even mentioned fighting you, you threw hands right then and there. Who in the world gets told by someone to meet them after school and they wait? It was a joke to need prep time to throw blows. If you were stupid enough to warn someone you deserved the beat down you got. You know how we knew someone wanted to fight us? When we were fighting them.

Anyone who took the time to breakdown why they were mad at you, what they planned to do to you, and hype a crowd up were perpetrators. What they were really doing was trying to call your bluff to save face, not put in work. They wanted to fight less than you did.

While Tamira was my introduction to the streets, academia introduced itself to me by means of Christ The King pre-K via Ms. Barber. It was a rough start, to say the least. I had just gotten over my fear of fighting only to be faced with another milestone. The knife I took to school to kill Chucky nearly got me suspended. Everyone at school had seen the movie and were all convinced he was going to come the next day. This was how the mind of 4 and 5-year-olds operated. We decided to be prepared. One person agreed to bring a pillowcase. Another, duct tape. Then there was the rope. I was the knife. Chucky's reign of terror had to end. I don't know why our parents even allowed us to watch that movie.

Kindergarten found me with Ms. Dr. Freeman at Rozelle Elementary. Yes, we called her the entire name at our young ages. It was a lot. To this day I hold her in high regard as a teacher. She was extremely patient and worked hands-on with both students and parents. This being back when parents were more active in their children's learning.

For the most part, I've always been an independent learner. My grandma would sit at the table with me after school and help me with reading, spelling, and math, again, because my parents were around but not involved. She was convinced I would be a teacher or attorney because I was studious and had a passion for helping others. I didn't just care about animals. People in need held a special place in my heart also. Sharda, one of my homegirls, couldn't read until we got to 6th grade. I spent days upon days tutoring her, encouraging her. For some sick reason, instead of building up those who could use the support, we down them. Calling academically challenged children 'stupid' in jest was the norm. This seeped into their subconscious, encouraging behavior fitting of the label.

One of my strongest characteristics was put into play early on: independence. I started walking to school and catching the RTA around 6-years-old, whenever my granddad could not drive me. He knew I was young so he made the greatest effort he could, but sometimes he just couldn't. It was a tender age to brave the streets of East Cleveland alone, but he wasn't up to it and my grandma never learned how so she hadn't driven a day in her life. They married when she was 18-years-old and he took her everywhere she needed to go or she caught the RTA as she did before they met.

Their relationship was the type people dream of growing old together and achieving. I admire what they built. They didn't need verbal communication. They knew each other through and through so they simply fed off of each other's movements and worked based on habits. He came home to a steaming hot plate of food every night without fail. She would carry his dinner up to the bedroom where he was watching his shows, and place it on a dinner tray in front of him. I remember there always had to be salt and pepper on the tray for him because no matter how she seasoned the food he needed it just in case.

The kicker for me was, my granddad was missing all of his teeth, but insisted on buying all of the candy when I brought the fundraiser packets from school: anything to support me. He would sit there and gum the gummy bears to death! You could hear the saliva in his mouth. It was the juiciest sound I ever heard. When the tins were empty he would keep one to hold the quarters he rationed out for my school snacks. Each night he left case quarters on the dresser for me to get little things I liked to munch on throughout the day. I knew where he kept it which meant I pilfered a few. He knew it and never said anything. Grandparents know it all. I could do no wrong. When the tin delivered up its last coin I lamented. Granddad hilariously reminded me my shenanigans were the reason I ran out so fast.

I needed my quarters. The corner stores accepted my two round offerings greedily in exchange for a soda and bag of hot fries, hot popcorn, chocolate fudge pops, orange creamsicles, or any variety of penny candy: banana being my favorite. It's a wonder I have teeth to this day with the mountain of Laffy Taffys and Now and Laters I devoured. My grandma made sure I never missed a dentist appointment because of my addiction to candy. She wanted to take preventative measures to ensure any cavities were caught ahead of time. Guess my granddad's toothless mouth was enough of a warning. I had to brush day and night, plus floss, to keep her and the dentist happy. I'm glad I did.

So yeah, my granddad was cool as a fan. He never raised a fuss. Just sat back and observed unless things got out of hand. His Burnette's gin was kept in a combination lockbox no one bothered. We all knew better. He'd take a shot and strike a Kool cigarette while he was dressing to step out. If his day was hard, he'd take a swig and sit at the foot of the joined twin beds.

I loved my grandma too. I did. It was just a different relationship. My granddad was my best friend growing up. He was a man of very few words so when people came with the questions about his gray eyes, they left with them. If it wasn't your business it didn't become your business by speaking with him. He was the representation of a man to me, standing a little over six feet tall wrapped in dark brown skin. You wouldn't catch him slipping when he stepped out. His freshly pressed slacks and shirt were accessorized by silk socks, dress shoes, a handkerchief, and a top hat. No one could say he didn't have style or looked like a slob. My grandparents took pride in how they carried themselves.

Reminiscing about him made me realize even more about my own self. I held to the preference of tall, dark men over lighter men all my life without knowing why. It dawns on me now my adversity to lighter men stems from my father being light. Conversely, my affinity for tall, dark men was birthed from my respect and adoration of my granddad.

Of course, Granddad and I didn't just step out fresh to death. We did other things together, like fish. He would take me out on Lake Eerie in a small boat he rented. We didn't do it often, but I remember the bluegills we caught and cleaned at home. That was the only part of it I remember. He didn't allow me to scale them, but I rinsed them and took credit for the cleaning anyway. I was far too young to scale fish. We would have been gagging on scales all night if I had.

These were just a few of his ways to let me know I mattered. He made it a point to spend quality time with me. Driving me to school, watching random shows, and sitting down to have conversations ensuring I was good were the simple things which made all the difference. It reinforced my security and sense of worth.

Speaking of quality time, I shared the bed with my grandparents until I reached 12-years-old. Thinking back on it, that was a long time. I should have been out of their bed years prior. They had two twin beds they joined together in the center of the room and I slept smack in the middle. Lucky for me, I was their baby and they were beyond the age of intercourse so they never put me out. Not even when I wet the bed, which I did for years.

"Gotdamn! You peed on my nightgown!" Would be the only complaint from my grandma. The sheer pink gown was her favorite and what she slept in most often. I don't know how my granddad seemed to escape my streams of urine. I was prohibited from drinking right before bedtime, but I managed to wet the bed anyway. This was simply just another reason my bond with them was so strong.

Being up under them all of the time guaranteed I picked up on some of their habits. I guess this is why people say I have an old soul. Smoking cigarettes was the only detrimental one, yet it was the earliest. My granddad preferred Salem 100s and I snuck them from his packs before I started sneaking from anyone else's. Eventually, and naturally, my grandma's packs got hit next. If I couldn't get away with getting one of theirs at the moment, I rolled grass in paper from the mail. Clearly, I was young and dumb. I never got caught though. The entire house smoked so if I smelled like it no one's suspicion was peaked. I would hang out of a window behind closed doors and spark one. Oh to be young and foolish.

While I formed an addiction at home, infatuation formed at school. Kindergarten held more for me than the foundation of my academic learning. It held my first crush and my first kiss, Christopher Hayes. A little light skinned boy whose round head framed two adorable dimples, Chris's presence became a lifelong one. He was the boy in my life, which many of us had at some point, who pulled their pants down and forced us to touch their penis. I was disturbed. A feeling of disgust and discomfort seized me on the alphabet carpet that day in class. I continued to know him and his family through the years, though our elementary romance eventually fizzled out.

He was replaced by Brandon. I made it my business to find a way to his house on my way home from Rozelle Elementary almost every day. Brandon had a strong resemblance to Usher and had anyone paid a penny for my thoughts on him they would have gotten their money's worth for sure.

I started becoming increasingly conscious of my appearance. These fledgling crushes created an awareness of what boys liked. As the grades progressed, their interests developed. One thing was clear: boys liked hair. Bald headed girls were constantly the target of ridicule and seldom got the attention they wanted.

Jamiel took on the responsibility of doing hair in our family, if we let him. He wasn't a professional, he just enjoyed styling hair. Appearances seriously mattered to him. This sparked an entire undercurrent of concern regarding his sexuality. For some reason I'll never understand, my family allowed him to put a perm in my hair when I was six. Needless to say, this unprofessionally, out of the box, home application of Just For Me left my hair flowing down the drain instead of on my scalp where I preferred it. You would think they banned him from my hair care. Nope. My family continued to allow him to install weaves and other styles on me. He was never bomb at what he did, but he eventually became good. The family's concerns regarding his sexuality would be confirmed in the following years, but family is family for us. It made no difference.

With everyone doing their part to make sure I looked presentable, I wore a neatly creased uniform and penny loafers with an actual shiny penny in them every day. Grandma wouldn't be caught dead letting me out of the house looking less than beautiful and well kept. My face, copper and shiny from grease, matched the penny in my loafers. As I walked out of the door, I deposited the two case quarters from the nightstand left out for me in my pocket for safe keeping.

Even though I was provided everything I needed, a desire to get what I wanted for myself blossomed within me at a very young age. My enterprising spirit introduced itself when I was 6-years-old. I had been pondering a plan to earn income, but we all know it takes money to make money. I needed an investor so I called the person I felt controlled the family's purse strings, aunt Genie. It was actually great practice for me because the conversation was structured the way any business/investor conversation is. She asked for the purpose of the loan and I promised her a return on her investment. The arrangement was very comfortable for me since she was the one I went to when I wanted or needed things anyway.

The following day she delivered the requested twenty dollars to me on her way to work, which I immediately headed to Finast with. Finast was our community grocery store. The employees knew your family and you knew theirs. I was filled with purpose the entire two-mile walk to the store, imaging each step of the process as I had been since conjuring the whole idea up. I had been sent to Finast by my grandma to pick up items before so I was familiar with the layout. After a good thirty minutes in the store, I stepped outside with my bags and hailed a taxi. They weren't real taxis. Just people soliciting to take you where you needed to go so you didn't have to catch the bus, but we called them taxis since they served the exact same purpose. I gave the driver my address, eager to get home and prepare for my bake sale.

Upon arriving, I paid the driver, bounced out of the vehicle and darted inside the house. Grandma agreed to help me with the cupcakes and other treats. The first day of the sale was a hit. I made one hundred fifty dollars and paid my aunt thirty dollars. Profit agreed with me so I wanted to see how far this could go. I returned to Finast the following day and expanded my menu to include foot long hot dogs, lemonade, and a few other popular items. I even hired two kids to hold signs to attract passing cars, two kids to take a wagon of items to sell to the dope boys, and two kids to sell door to door. Dope boys made for the best customers because they stayed posted at their stations slinging product for days at a time. We called their clothes 'trap' clothes because they were in them for so long. They needed to eat but had limited mobility. Dope boys loved seeing the wagon come their way. Business was good for the entire summer.

As the weather started changing, I didn't want to be outside hustling. I convinced Grandma to sell dinners during the winter. She agreed and made a good profit. Since she did the cooking, I did the running. I went to Green's Barbershop, nail salons, Rite Aid, Renee's Cleaner, and Chris's Car Shop to deliver orders. People in our community preferred home cooked meals and looked forward to purchasing the dinners. They sold quickly, keeping my grandma in the kitchen more than usual. She didn't complain though. The extra income was welcome. She enjoyed refraining from accepting money from aunt Genie whenever she could.

> **EVEN THOUGH I WAS PROVIDED EVERYTHING I NEEDED, A DESIRE TO GET WHAT I WANTED FOR MYSELF BLOSSOMED WITHIN ME AT A VERY YOUNG AGE.**

This period in my life formed my love for soul food and a good spades or dominoes game. Often, when I dropped orders off a game would be in play. All the screaming, slamming of cards on the table, profanity and theatrics were just my style. I'd hang back for a few minutes and look at people's hands, paid attention to how they playe,d and watched the table. I noticed how they counted cards and communicated non-verbally with their partners. I wanted to try my hand at it but they were serious about their games and told me to start practicing with my friends.

Once I got a taste of entrepreneurship, and the income it produced, I was hooked. My mind constantly procured the means of generating revenue. I paid attention to what the adults and children around me spoke about, purchased, pastimes, and desires. If people were into it, I could manipulate it to my benefit.

Back in school, learning and hustling weren't the curriculum. Fighting had become the agenda of the day at Rozelle when I got to 2nd grade. By this time I had overcome my fear of squaring up. Fear is a key reason many people lose fights. It makes them hold back and doubt themselves instead of letting loose and fully defending themselves. Fear makes them apprehensive. But 2nd grade introduced me to some beastly children. The majority of my peers were bad as hell. They acted up and fought non-stop.

There was a girl named Kelly I remember no one liked. The only two things I remember about her was how disliked she was and how much she got jumped on. It was like…all the time. She wasn't the only one. Everyone got tried. Things got to a point where our teacher, Ms. Osbourne, got so tired of it she taped paper from the floor to the ceiling in order to block her desk in a corner, separating her from assaults.

We had another girl named Rostia in the class who looked as if she belonged to a family of sharecroppers. Tall, big, and tar baby black, she looked as disadvantaged as she was. Her unimaginably nappy hair reminded you of cotton puffs. Rostia was obnoxiously annoying, so the bully in me felt obliged to do something about it. I chased her home often. She never bucked back. She kowtowed to me and did everything in her power to befriend me. When she invited me over to her house, I would go. Mainly just to have something to do. Her parents were never anywhere around, but also my Usher look-a-like crush lived on her block. Seeing him was an incentive.

My days kicking it with Rostia were short lived. A dog got loose on her block and almost bit me. I loved dogs and had vicious ones of my own, but there is a huge difference between your dogs and unfamiliar dogs. I wasn't about to chance giving that dog another opportunity to taste my hind parts so I stuck with seeing Rostia at school.

> ONCE I GOT A TASTE OF ENTREPRENEURSHIP, AND THE INCOME IT PRODUCED, I WAS HOOKED.

Ashley Rox was a new addition to Rozelle shortly before the school year ended. Where most of us had grown up in the neighborhood together, she was an outsider. I didn't care who she was though. I was so used to saying whatever I wanted and treating people however I felt like treating them. You could say I had gotten a bit out of control. Our classes had those old school tablet arm desk with the basket underneath for your books and notebooks. One day, I was leaning back against my seat, lifting the front two legs off the floor. Whatever the teacher was saying obviously didn't have my attention. There was a bookshelf behind the desk I sat in at the end of the row. Ashley had been saying something, not to me, but I made it about me. For no reason at all, I interjected, "Bitch yo momma!" Well, Ashley promptly turned around in her chair and punched me square in the nose. I never saw it coming. I always told people to ask about me, but maybe I should have asked about Ashley! It took me completely off guard. I may have even lost a second or two between the punch and my realization of what occurred. That hit sent me flying backwards out of my chair against the bookshelf. I got up, holding my nose, leaking blood like a dripping faucet. It was the first time, and one of the very few, I had been beaten up. What an experience. There wasn't even a fight afterward.

Aside from the fights, Cleveland brought new excitement to its residents, and hope for cash flow from tourist in the early 1990s. Cleveland won a bid against multiple states to house the Rock and Roll Hall of Fame Museum. Most of the kids in my school didn't listen to Rock and Roll. We knew some of the major names like Aerosmith, Red Hot Chili Peppers, and Nirvana, but that's it. Not many of us visited. Some did, mostly during field trips. It wasn't something we connected with, just something to do.

Ms. Davis took over as my educator for my 3rd grade year. She was a decent enough white lady. Her curls were always pulled back, showing off a conservatively powered face. Her moderation saved her. She would've been eaten alive coming up in there with a carnival face. Ms. Davis stood out to me because she was the first teacher who saw beyond my behavioral issues and recognized my intelligence.

Ms. Davis advised the administration I was the best reader in her class so one day a few of them entered and called my name to come with them. My peers started howling and cracking jokes, believing I was being sent to a remedial reader's class. In reality, I was hand selected to read some facts about Michael Jackson over the P.A. system after the pledge of allegiance. It being Black History Month, the school was supposed to guess the black celebrity's identity without me saying the actual name. Whoever got it right first won a prize.

Ms. Davis's class was also the first class I can recall expressing any type of creativity in. She showed us how to craft books by covering cardboard with construction paper, cut to size. I was stoked. This was my first experience with crafting a book. Who knew it wouldn't be my last?

Across the hall from Ms. Davis's class was Ms. Tober's 6th grade class. My cousin Doozer was in Ms. Tober's class. We would meet up in the hall when school let out to walk home together. He lived one block up from me so it was cool. We didn't know much about each other except we were cousins so it seemed the thing to do to try to build some form of a bond. But that was it. Our households didn't socialize so it was school and the walk home for us.

I may not have had a relationship with each member of my family, but the family I knew made sure they were all I needed. Aunt Genie and Jamiel stepped up to the plate, providing my grandparents with the income to care for my mother and myself. It was because of their generous sponsorship I was able to enjoy Christmases, new uniforms, clothes every time the seasons changed, field trips, and the occasional toy. My closet was updated constantly with the latest name brands: Jordans were a favorite. I can't say I ever experienced need. I'll be forever grateful for the village which raised me.

I also spent most of my younger years with my cousin Keisha. We were like sisters. Like any pair or group that spends a substantial amount of time together, there is always going to be a dominant one. I was it. Keisha was quiet and a follower. She rarely initiated anything and was glad to go along with a game plan presented to her. I will never, ever forget when I convinced her drinking urine increased your strength. She fell for it and drank a chapstick cap of mine. I worried later she would tell and I would get my ass beat. I did.

Keisha lived in Parkside Gardens, an apartment complex on 260th and Euclid. Cleveland apartments were a little different. These were six stories with ten or twenty units on each floor. Keisha lived on one of the higher ones which used to excite me as a child. I don't know why. Children typically just enjoyed being high up in buildings.

The community of apartments consisted of about three buildings with a swimming pool in the center. The pool was normally the meetup spot and it was definitely where everyone hung in the summer. Speaking of that, I still have a fear of swimming from when Keisha and I went to the pool at her complex. Keisha was a confident swimmer. She spent a lot of time at pools and learned to swim when she was young. I, on the other hand, had not. She knew I couldn't swim so she told me she would protect me and put me on her back so I could be with her in the deep end. Somehow I slipped off. Probably because I was moving too much or she wasn't big enough to carry me. Of course, she got me out of the water, but the experience of almost drowning and the notion that I could die had me like, *Nope. No more water for me.* It's crazy because now at thirty-one I will go kayaking and white water rafting, yet I can't tread water. I guess I never mastered buoyancy.

Aside from hanging at the pool, we frequented a vacant field next to the apartment complex and the woods in front of them. We searched the trees many times during our childhood for the witch neighborhood children believed lived deep inside. According to them, she ran out to the tree line to snatch any children alone at night. They also claimed to have heard her cackling once or twice. I don't think we truly believed a witch resided there because I doubt we would have ventured there if we did. It was more likely the thrill of doing it.

The field was a different matter. Naturally, with us constantly being together, I pulled her into my hustles. Making money stayed on my mind. Keisha and I would strategize ways to transform the field into a useful location, like a park. I think selling things was the original means to that end, but I can't remember now. The complex itself had a beautiful landscape with perennials. Joyce, the building's manager, would be pissed when she caught us engaging in our other hustle, pulling up those pretty perennials and selling them door to door. We tried to avoid getting caught, but it was what it was. Once she caught us she kept watch for us. We still managed to pick the place bare. The profits from the flowers were supposed to get us the field for our park.

I will never forget a couple answering the door with, "Awww, so cute!" and buying several bouquets. They seemed so in love. Couples like them were easy marks. They were always up for getting tokens of affection. As soon as we ran into them we kicked the charm up a notch. We didn't have to say much, the flowers sold themselves. All we had to do was smile hard and say all the 'thank yous' we had in us.

I specifically targeted lone males. They either had someone at home or were interested in someone. Even boys my age got approached.

"I know you got a girl." I would say. You alleged they had girlfriends, whether they did or not, because all guys like the idea of having the girl they had their eye on. "Girls like flowers. Get her some of these." If they had money on them I had the sale.

Believe it or not, there was a downside to going home with full pockets. Keisha's mom indulged in drugs with my mom so when we returned to the apartment they would normally be chilling. My assumption is they did them together. By the time Keisha and I got inside, her mom would be frying onion rings from scratch. They didn't have a lot of money so this was a cheap food item.

Our mothers knew what we had been doing, so without fail my mom would say, "Oh you made some money? Go buy me some cigarettes."

I hated them asking us for money. We were the ones out hustling all day just for them to find little ways to take everything we made. Weren't they the parents? Shouldn't they be taking care of us and letting us enjoy our earnings? Saving the money I made for my goals was why I did what I did. Without an ounce of guilt, my answer was always, "No." Unfortunately, my mother had a terrible habit of speaking to me and cursing me out as if I were an adult when I didn't do what she wanted.

She would immediately fly into, "Bitch fuck you! I don't want your motherfucking money anyway!" She used to talk crazy to me. Then I'd get hit with the, "You little dick sucking bitch." This was her go to because I always had full lips. I don't know why my lips bothered her so much. What did she expect? I was the product of her and my father. She had to know the chances of that feature expressing itself. I grew into them, but they were fuller than most when I was younger. Mind you, at my age fellatio was foreign to me, but she was so messed up in the mind from the drugs she had no clue what she was saying. It was really messed up. If I thought more highly of her back then I would have been hurt. Instead, I felt irritated and angry.

Another tactic of hers was a molestation allegation against my cousin Jamiel. All I could think was, *What the hell is wrong with her*? I have no memories of anything she said happened. I know people say you may suppress traumatic events or I may have been too young to remember, but no. This didn't occur.

> **SHE WOULD IMMEDIATELY FLY INTO, "BITCH FUCK YOU! I DON'T WANT YOUR MOTHERFUCKING MONEY ANYWAY!" SHE USED TO TALK CRAZY TO ME. THEN I'D GET HIT WITH THE, "YOU LITTLE DICK SUCKING BITCH."**

It blew me she would just recklessly throw these rumors out there when severe criminal charges could have been brought against him for these false accusations. She could have ruined his life if someone took her seriously. I couldn't wrap my mind around it. The shit was crazy to me.

PILLARS

I was never under the impression we were rich growing up. I knew we weren't poor, still, I heard my fair share of 'nos' due to our limited resources. My granddad received a pension from his days with Nickel Plate Railroad, another major historical piece of Cleveland's past, and he ran numbers on the side. All that barely kept the bills paid. My grandmother did a stint at General Electric and cleaned homes for white families when they needed extra cash before I was born, but for the most part, she devoted her life to taking care of her family and home.

Alice Ruth Hutchins was a fierce, strong woman. Everyone referred to her by her middle name, Ruth. She didn't take anything from anyone and she never waited for someone to do anything for her. If you said you would pick her up at 8:00 a.m. to take her to the grocery store and 7:50 a.m. arrived without you, she headed for the bus. On any day you could catch her with a 40 oz of Cream Ale beer paired with a fresh pack of Winston 100's, situated in her white, shell back chair on the front porch. She kept a watchful eye on the street so she knew everyone and their business. If she had put her mind to it, she could have run a successful gossip column in the local paper.

Though she loved to see everything, she wasn't keen on being seen. She hid her mysterious gray eyes behind tinted shades. Even still, she was a difficult beauty to miss. The questions regarding her pedigree were incessant. Had her eye color been brown or black, her parents' race wouldn't have been on everyone's mind. Interrogations about your DNA get old quick. The Jheri curl she kept short was dyed auburn so frequently you forgot it wasn't her natural color. It worked well with her reddish-brown tone, making her glow. She even made sure her frames were of an auburn tint to match her hair. Like my granddad, she was about looking sharp. No wonder they were attracted to each other.

When she smiled you were in for another surprise. An open-faced gold tooth drew your gaze to a row of pristine whites. Weird fact, she bragged on her gold tooth. She would go on and on about it being real gold compared to the knock off, gold-plated fronts and caps the younger generations were rocking. The story behind how she got it was what threw me. Her parents allowed her to get it at 14-years-old in her hometown of Atlanta. I felt fourteen was very young. She explained they were different times.

So while she sat pretty, observing the neighborhood from our porch, I was delegated with the task of running notes to the owner of the nearby corner store, showing permission to purchase her beer and cigarettes. "You get lost?" She would ask if I hadn't come straight back. From time to time I bumped into one of my friends at the store coming or going and momentarily forget the task at hand. We were kids and fun was a priority. She never really minded. I think she actually factored it in. In fact, if I wasn't around, a neighborhood dope boy would gladly run the errand in my place. They normally stayed focused and came straight back. Most elders in the community had called on them from time to time for assistance. You could even catch them carrying groceries or laundry from the bus stop for them. Elderly and churches were their Achilles heel.

Being her age and from her era, my grandma had very strict rules. There was no spending the night or eating at anyone else's house. Once or twice my charm won me a sleepover at a friend's. That was it. I was taught streetlights had no business beating you home, and you needed to be dressed by 8 a.m. because she didn't' believe in laying around the house undressed.

You were required to bathe at the beginning of the day and at the conclusion without exception. One bath per day was unacceptable. Many people would consider that extreme and say it caused an unnecessary increase in the water bill. For most families, one bath either in the morning or evening was good enough. If you smelled tangy, having already bathed for the day, a bird bath to hit your hotspots would suffice. Not for Ruth. A bird bath was synonymous

> **SO WHILE SHE SAT PRETTY, OBSERVING THE NEIGHBORHOOD FROM OUR PORCH, I WAS DELEGATED WITH THE TASK OF RUNNING NOTES TO THE OWNER OF THE NEARBY CORNER STORE, SHOWING PERMISSION TO PURCHASE HER BEER AND CIGARETTES.**

with a hoe bath and there were no hoes in her house so your entire ass had to get in the tub! A welcoming bar of Lever 2000 waited for you each time you entered the bathroom. Oh! But once my grandma got a taste of Dove it was the only soap to enter the house.

Our house had the old-fashioned, deep porcelain tub perched on four legs. Capacity: one. It was positioned beside the toilet, behind the sink. Bathing was the only option. There was no showering apparatus. The funny thing is, back then these tubs were considered ugly and found mostly in poorer homes. Now, they are vintage, popular décor.

Walking around the house in white socks was also forbidden. Not even on the red carpet. When I did, she'd scrub them so vigorously with her knuckles you would have thought they were from a brand-new pack. Those years of cleaning for white people definitely made her a magician with housework. "Even carpet holds dirt baby. You just don't see it." She swore by Tide laundry detergent to the point it was the only detergent I trusted for a while into adulthood. I never saw the results of anything else. It's all she washed with. She required me to wear house shoes. You could never get me to believe dirt was able to cross survive in our home.

The woman never stopped cleaning. Germs weren't her only concern. Pests were attracted to bacteria and dirt. We bombed the house a few times a year due to roaches. Although our home was nearly spotless we were still susceptible to the occasional episode. It was a task. Everything in the kitchen cabinet would get removed or covered with old newspapers and sheets. We didn't have a rodent infestation, thankfully, but they made their way in from time to time. Our tactic was wooden mouse traps laced with peanut butter. If you weren't careful they would remove your finger when you set them.

She was like most old black women: a white sectional imprisoned in plastic, walls with their red and white dressing, and glass tables which were never to be touched. The house was actually a duplex. The other side remained unoccupied in case someone in the family needed to live there. My uncle took it over on and off with his girlfriend, as did my mom, Deedee. 'Mom', was difficult for me to say when referring to her. It wasn't out of a refusal to acknowledge her, or even out of resentment for her absence in my life. Titles are relational. 'Mom' didn't fit the relationship we shared and she embarrassed me. To this day she asks me why I insisted on calling her Deedee. I think by now she knows.

Her age group lived by one more thing, aside from hygiene and family. Superstitions were also a serious thing for us. You were never to let someone sweep your feet with a broom or you'd be cursed. Purses should never be left on the floor or you'd be broke. Splitting a pole was an invitation for bad luck in your life. Allowing more than one person at a time to do your hair promoted hair loss.

In addition, zodiac signs and horoscopes determined how you viewed people, what you expected from them, and who was a good match or definite bad pairing. Even now, while I've abandoned some of the beliefs from my upbringing, zodiac signs have always proven true so I maintained my faith in them. Not quite the hoodoo and voodoo of the bayou, but it was our way of life. I grew up abiding by these taboos.

So yeah, I started hustling young, I came from a real ass family, and I could handle myself in the streets even at my young age. There was still more to me. Making money was an ambition, not what I loved. When I was born two old poodles, Pearie and Champagne, were part of the household. They provided the energetic companionship a house full of elderly didn't. One was killed violently by our next door neighbor's dog and one died slowly of old age.

I was too young to remember them. All I have left are old Polaroids of me playing with them. I do however remember the neighbor whose dog killed Champagne. Her name was Jewel, a little old white lady. I mention Jewel being white because there were no other whites left in the neighborhood. You might have been able to scare up two or three, but they were scarce. She had one son who was slightly darker than her so we knew for sure he was black.

The only other one I remember was Mrs. Barry. That was up for debate though because people argued she was just so light you confused her for white. Either way, the dope boys walked her home and carried her groceries as they did for all the elders of the community.

Jewel was cordial with my grandma and her grown resident son befriended my uncle Terry. I don't know why Jewel took to me, most likely she was just old and lonely, but she would invite me over for these disgusting pineapple and cottage cheese snacks. The pineapples were fine; the cottage cheese threw me for a loop. I ate it to make Jewel happy. My grandma felt she was harmless. Trust and believe that's the only reason she allowed me to keep her company. I never let on, but I anticipated the visits as much as her. She'd also would carry me along with her to Mt. Nebo Monastery Baptist Church on Superior from time to time. Church has always been and will always be a staple of the black community. If your parents weren't taking you, someone would pick up the responsibility. They acted like if they racked up enough referrals, they had a better chance of gaining entry into heaven.

The loss of our poodles created a need to fill the void they left. We missed having dogs in the home. As a dog lover, I was thrilled to receive Baby Face and Rebel. These two I remember. I loved them. We had the rottweilers for around eight to twelve years. Baby Face and I had the type of bond a girl should have with her dog. He'd lay beside me, he was the first at the door when I got home from school, and it was he who followed my every step in the house. Anytime I played my saxophone, he howled to the melody. No one understood my dogs like me. My cousin Elithia told me I was nasty when she saw me feeding them from the same fork I was eating from. I told her I felt they were human just like us. I'm proud to announce I no longer share utensils with my fur babies.

Rebel got his name from his aggressive behavior. For this reason, none of the strays I tried to incorporate into the household after them lasted. The pit bull we traded for paper food stamps seemed to stand a chance until he was shot in the head by the police. My mom said they treated him like he was a black man. The neighbors snitched because he kept getting out of the yard and had the nerve to refer to him as a threat. He wasn't. He never even approached them. They just saw him loose in our yard and were afraid. The police arrived on the scene, riddled him with bullets, then left without any consideration for the family.

The strays I constantly brought home drove my grandma insane. One we even tried to abandon at a local park. Thing is, with it being a 'local' park and all, he found his way home. Dogs tend to do that. Weirdly enough, one day I noticed I hadn't been seeing him. I never found out what happened to him. He was there one day and gone the next. Grandma never answered any questions regarding his whereabouts. She is still a suspect in his disappearance.

Hazel, a neighborhood street dog, had a litter of puppies under a fence by Pork Chop's house. I stumbled upon them after hearing barely audible whimpers in the abandoned field near the fence. My initial route was going to take me to the corner store for some candy. That changed immediately. I gathered my new babies to carry them home. I was so ecstatic my heart was bubbling over and my feet barely touched the ground until I hit the front porch.

My biggest supporter, Grandma, sat up with me countless nights bottle feeding the eleven puppies while we waited for good homes to become available. None ever did. The home we delivered them to, unwillingly on my end, was the shelter. It ate me alive. Thankfully I still had my rotts at home for comfort. It meant a lot she even let me rescue them in the first place. She allowed several untrained puppies in her sanitary home. She knew how much I loved them. She did it all for me.

We kept Rebel away from the puppies while they were there. We were concerned about how he would react to them. Uncle Terry was the only one Rebel allowed in his personal space. He was super aggressive so no one even felt comfortable getting close to him. Baby Face, on the other hand, didn't show aggression unless someone showed it against me. He gave you a chance. Neither of them let people who were not related to me too close though. My family even had to be careful. It was hard for anyone to spank me with them around. Baby Face and Rebel had to be taken outside when I had to be disciplined.

There was this one time my mom tried spanking me. I didn't have much respect for her as a disciplinarian so I offered her my middle finger and fled into the adjoining basement. In an attempt to apprehend me, she ran around the front of the house to cut me off. Her attempt was foiled by my protectors who stood growling between us.

My bodyguards kept me safe for the majority of my childhood until Rebel was lost to cancer and Baby Face was euthanized when he could no longer walk. While I was willing to add more dogs to the family when they were alive, I lost interest when they died. Uncle Terry brought Shaba, a beautiful Lab/Pit mix, home for Babyface when we lost Rebel, in hopes of keeping his spirit up. He was getting older and the loss of his brother weighed on him.

My dogs weren't my only protectors. Granddad stood guard between me and any beatings. His raspy voice would demand anyone coming my way with punishment to, "Leave that girl alone!"

I can't count how many whippings he rescued me from. I know it burned them up inside sometimes when they felt I really deserved one. Between my dogs and my granddad, I was untouchable.

To be honest, I know I deserved most of the whippings I didn't get. Perhaps if the rod hadn't been spared the rebellion of my following years would have been deterred. Rather, my own cognizance brought me the lessons which secured the life I live and appreciate today.

I still hear the raspy, "Leave that girl alone," when people come for me. I smile and my heart tells him, "I got this." If you heard us speak, you would think I inherited his voice. I didn't. He was in a traumatic accident when he was younger. His vocal cords were impacted, causing a strained, low, husky sound in place of what once was. Voices like ours were different. They made people stop and listen, even if what we were saying didn't.

There is one time of the year in particular where I miss them both so much I can't stand it. Christmas. Not for the gifts and the food, well, maybe the food a little. To make money during the holidays, grandma would clean everyone's chitterlings in the neighborhood for ten dollars per bucket, each bucket weighing ten pounds. We would stay up all night boiling and rinsing them out, then inspecting them to make sure they were clean. I hated the smell, but I did it because it meant I got to help the woman I adored. Spending time with her was everything to me. We even had a tradition of hopping on the bus every Friday to go shopping, which was especially enjoyable during Christmas when all of the lights were out and the streets were clogged with consumers dragging bags of overpriced sales items.

The family made sure each Christmas felt like a huge event. The house was abuzz with activity. I loved white Christmas trees, so each year one was pulled down from the attic from the previous year and redecorated. I would sit on the floor with the bulging box of tinsel, ornaments, and lights. We didn't bother much with placing items on the front yard, around the windows or lighting the house, but the tree, that got everything.

My grandparents allowed me to place decorations anywhere I wanted and helped with the spots I couldn't reach. We scattered candy canes throughout the branches and grandma let me help her bake cookies for the Santa I knew didn't exist.

However fun the holiday was, it was equally frustrating for the adults. I remember helping and watching my grandma prepare food days in advance, up to the hour of the main course for the day. No matter. She could have started it a month in advance there was always a hold-up. She ran out of this. The stores were closed so she had to find a way to improvise. Someone didn't make it and their dish was missing so she had to replace it.

Nobody could eat until everything was done. We would be super hungry and strictly denied until we could all sit together to bless the food and consume as a family. Try to slip into Ruth's kitchen to steal a bite here or nibble there and she would wound your soul with her tongue. She found it disrespectful and unsanitary. If she caught you in a pot those steel gray eyes would pierce through you while a "Hell Naw!" sounded the alarm.

The only one allowed in the kitchen with her on the day was Jamiel, sometimes. That was it. It didn't matter how much still needed to be done. Just Jamiel. Even if the food wasn't done until 9 p.m., which we saw happen more than one Christmas, she refused additional help. As a mother and wife now, I make it my business to have dinner ready on holidays by 1 p.m. It's important for the family to have time to eat, relax, and enjoy each other. If everyone is waiting for food the whole day it's not the same. We eat, sleep, and eat again at my house. This way, it is super chill and so much food is eaten throughout the day there are few to no leftovers cluttering the fridge.

Regarding what waited for me beneath my pretty tree, I always got something amazing. One year a pool table with a reverse side for table hockey was my favorite. The top two presents over all of those years were my Gateway desktop computer and instant Polaroid camera. I got on everyone's nerves with the camera. Everywhere I went for months, including around the house, I was snapping pics. Especially the Christmas I opened it. I was the family photographer for the rest of the day. Once everyone felt I had played with it enough I started hearing, "Ok now Ieshia. Put that thing away" or, "No! Don't take pictures of me." Depending on who it was, I would snap my shot anyway and hightail it out of there. The photos that meant the most to me were taped to the mirror in my bedroom.

My Gateway was the introduction to AOL and the whole 'You've Got Mail' wave. Instant messaging and being in chat rooms with strangers from all over the world was the thing; and looking back, I don't believe parents knew how dangerous this was. Your child was in the house at the moment, true. But predators and traffickers gained so much access to us without us realizing it. Man, it was wild for real. We would exchange information on where we lived, went to school, and details about ourselves that made us easy marks. We had no idea.

Slowly over the next few years, the community we knew transformed from a neighborhood to a hood. Drug dealers still had a level of honor and concern for elders, children, and churches, but as the quality of the community diminished so did that until it was gone. Before our very eyes gangs, drug trafficking, prostitution, unmaintained infrastructure, failing businesses, shootings, underfunded schools, and corrupt law enforcement ravaged what remained like termites. Today, Piru Blood Gang runs the top of the street, Folks took over the lower end where we lived, and various smaller rival groups were loosely scattered throughout nearby neighborhoods.

This wasn't the first shift our neighborhood experienced. One of the ugly truths about Cleveland is: its communities saw the extremes of both destitution and wealth. Euclid Avenue housed 'Millionaire's Row' or 'Showplace of America' in the early 1900s. This collection of mansions belonging to the elite of the nation were compared to landscapes and structures in Paris itself. Just how affluent was this community? John D. Rockefeller called it home. Most of the city's charitable donations to culture, infrastructure, education, and business came from these residents. They were the money. Unfortunately, the investments they made in the city caused a catch 22. While they were valuable changes, they inevitably drove up the cost of land and taxes. As Millionaire Row's elites relocated due to the effects of their own endeavors, their uninhabited homes were transformed into commercial properties and more. One such piece of property belonged to the founder of Standard Oil. Kirk Junior High, my middle school, was built in 1932 on land donated by Mr. Rockefeller.

Today, only four of the original streets remain. Stringent restrictions are in place on the homeowners on those blocks and they take extreme care of the community. None of the surviving structures are allowed to be altered in any way.

The fact that my school was a historic building played a major part in shaping my athleticism and the track victories my school achieved because we didn't have a track. No. We weren't lucky enough to have the same resources as suburban schools. We ran the steps inside the school or the track at the community center on Martin Luther King and Shaw Ave. While our races were for the 400-meters, the center's track was 440-meters on dirt, meaning our training incorporated an additional 40-meters and more difficult terrain. We definitely roughed it out. The result would be us smoking the daylights out of our suburban counterparts in competitions. Their ignorance and poor sportsmanship led them to taunt us, saying we could only outrace them because we had to run from crime and police in the inner city. They also accused our boys' team of looking too old to compete. Typical stereotype. Our builds were genetically larger and we didn't have the childish appearance afforded by stress-free lives. Life simply hits different when it's real.

In fact, we trained harder due to our lack of resources. We were damned if we did, damned if we didn't. Had we not trained harder, we would have been called lazy. Had we argued our lack of resources, we would have been told we made excuses. We earned every win so it didn't matter and our skin was tough being from where we were from so it didn't hurt.

Our coach, Mr. Rodney Brown, boasted about us all the time. Coach Brown had one of those super muscular upper bodies with large quads and a firm butt. His complexion was midnight black topped off with his box top fade. He looked like a retired marine. His technique was aggressive. You wouldn't know we were children from how he spoke to us and crying would get you just about kicked off of 'his' team. He trained winners, not whiners. Softer kids cracked under him. I remember the time he told a girl to stop running like she had a tampon in her. We erupted in laughter, but others may have been offended or embarrassed. We knew Coach though. We actually loved him.

Plus, Coach was the ISS, in school suspension, teacher. What this meant for our bad asses was if for any reason we found ourselves in ISS, we had to see his face. And while he didn't bring it up at the moment, as soon as we were at practice, he clowned us. Coach had no chill. He didn't do any of it to hurt us. It was his way of keeping us on track and making us rethink our decisions.

My peers from the suburbs who had encountered me on the track or on the court called me Action Jackson. They watched me work and knew I was a beast. My races were the 400-meter dash and the 4x4 anchor. To spice things up and stand out, I wore long black and red socks with black and red cleats at every race since they were our track team's colors.

My track victories were a source of pride for me. I begged my family to come out in support of me to see what I was capable of. All I got were 'next times'. Someone had to work, or didn't want to take the bus that far, or had other plans. I knew I was fortunate to have the family I did. I received more than most in our community. My family went out of their way so I never knew what it was like to go without. I never wanted to seem ungrateful or spoiled, but they were falling short in a major category in my life. It would have made a difference to me if I saw one of my people in the crowd cheering me on.

While society tried to enforce their stereotypes upon us, and break us at the same damn time, family dynamics were whittling away at my spirit as well. My maternal grandmother, Connie, thought I was more of a house servant than a grandchild. She fetched me on Fridays after school and put me to work around the house. I wish she hadn't. She made me hate weekends. See, what was happening here was she got a dose of Jesus and felt guilty for not being there for her own children so she tried to make up for it with her grands. The problem was she didn't treat us like treasured grands that got to run around, play and get spoiled.

Saturdays at her house included sweeping, dusting, mopping, and the scrubbing of her neck and back while she bathed. In my mind I'm thinking, *I should be home watching Saturday morning cartoons and running the streets.* Damn, I hated visiting her. As if that wasn't enough, on Sundays I would be outfitted in second or third-hand clothing and my bang fried with a hot comb in preparation for church. All the while she winning best dressed at church with the biggest hats and in perfect attendance for all church meetings or events. This was the type of black church people who aren't born into its culture fear. The one where service last nine hours, has four speakers, two collections, and an intercession. I ultimately informed my grandma that these visits were insufferable and she ended them for me.

My father's family didn't exert much effort in forging an authentic relationship with me either. I spent a brief period of my life with his sister LaLa on another part of Euclid until she adopted a family member's baby and moved to Vegas. Aunt LaLa was the only one who took an interest in me. She was a nurse and could afford to live in this really nice complex of green and white townhomes next to a park. It was a nice escape from the hood at the time.

As for the rest of his side of the family, my oldest sister got their affection. Selena's mom was Puerto Rican and the family loved her mixed appearance. Being biracial or having biracial children in the black community always seemed to be something of an accomplishment. They tried placating me with speeches on how loved I was and how we were all family and there were no favorites, but the truth is an undeniable feeling deep in your bones. I never felt bonded with them. Maybe that isn't even what hurt me. I think what really got to me was all the amazing, warm memories she had that I didn't. Perhaps I shouldn't have expected to have the same experience since I hadn't grown up with them as she had, but the distance I felt with them upset me. In a nutshell, all I had was the family that raised me.

MONEY MOVES

Instability in the economy continued to periodically affect the landscapes and culture of the city. Even now, with Cleveland being a blue-collar city, the majority of the jobs are white collar. What this means is white collars commute into the city to work, but don't reside there so the money they make doesn't get spent there either. The blue collars who live in the city can't find good paying jobs so there is no money being circulated in the communities and poverty continues.

Police posted up like street thugs, clocking the movements of drug dealers all day. That was their agenda. Not protecting or serving, not ensuring the safety of the residents. They knew what the dealers were moving and what they were making. When the sun laid itself to rest, the uniformed bandits would relieve them of their cut under the bridge and release them back on the block. Business as usual. And, crazy as it sounds, the world would have made more sense to me had all of them been white. I would have expected the exploitation from them. But these were black cops harassing their own. Not trying to mentor or save them; just encouraging the cycle of destruction in black families and communities for their own meager gain.

Our duplex was removed enough from it that I didn't see any of this out of my own front window, but I was still close enough to know those personally affected or to hear it on the daily. Though I didn't grow up in the projects I was often in and around them. My cousins Joe, Stephone, Kenyatta, and Deanna lived in Ottawa projects off of 30th. It was typical, with its cinder block walls and tile floors covered in roaches and filth, harboring destitution.

True to self, I loved it. Being in these environments thrilled me. There was so much to do and so many other children to play with. Families without money seemed to have the best snacks. I can't remember the brand, I just know my cousins kept this one cereal I made it my business to eat. I mean, whatever had the highest sugar content was in their cabinets. Cookie Crisp, Froot Loops, Fruity Pebbles…you name it! The only cereals my grandma allowed in the house were Frosted Flakes with fresh or chopped bananas, Cheerios or King Vitamin. So, as you can imagine, I couldn't wait to get to the good stuff at my cousins' house.

I smile when I think back on those days with them in the ghetto; in particular, scraping by to survive. Only able to get things on sale and sharing everything they could with each other to make things stretch. My joy in these memories stems from where they are now. See, the hood will either elevate or bury you. They soared. Their mother strove to achieve a better life for her children. Little did she know, they watched her ambition and perseverance every step of the way. They all wound up successful in their careers and she owns several businesses. A perfect example that the only limitations you have are the ones you place upon yourself.

The inner city shared similar characteristics, challenges, and events. The inner city differs from the project slightly. Projects are always apartments, often funded by government assistance. The inner city consisted of government subsidized residences and personally owned homes. No matter which area you called home, East Cleveland smelled of beer, smog, and BBQ. No one had to turn on the television to watch a good fight. All you had to do was venture outside and wait. One was bound to take place sooner or later. Violence and crime abounded.

A tragedy shook our community in 1994: the murder of Bianca White. She was found stabbed to death in her home on Penrose Ave. while doing homework. Her mother stated Bianca had asked to be picked up from school. Her mother's schedule made it impossible. That ate her alive. Had she picked her baby up from school, she would still be alive. Who can understand the guilt she felt? How terrified must Bianca have been, home alone, assaulted and bleeding to death? Who was this murderer in our community? What motivated the thirty-eight puncture wounds to her small frame? Parents were on edge for a while after this. Everyone promised to keep watch for each other's children if they had to work late. Latchkey children were always left unattended while single parents, or both parents, worked long or late hours to barely break even. It robbed us of the ability to feel secure within our own homes. The authorities opined the killer had to be someone Bianca knew due to evidence discovered in their investigation, which is ongoing to this day.

Parents became increasingly aware of who their children played had around them from that point forward. Thankfully, I kept the same company for years. Ketra was my best friend. All of us children in the neighborhood teased her by calling her Ketchup because of how her name rolled off of our inexperienced tongues. She took it in good humor. Her vibe matched my vibe better than our other friends. The only person I didn't prefer over her was Keisha. She was blood. Ketra and I conjured up business ideas, shared secrets, fought each other's battles, and refused to hang out with anyone the other didn't like. Yeah, pretty much like Keisha and I, except we weren't related.

We found our way to Hot Sauce Williams every chance we got with our dollar and twenty-five cents for an order of fries with sauce. You couldn't find fries like this anywhere else. They were fresh cut with a family barbecue sauce that sat in your mouth long after the fries were gone.

Eugene 'Hot Sauce' Williams entered the BBQ world in 1934 and expanded his dream into a small chain of local restaurants with his family's signature mix of molasses, ketchup, and vinegar. People loved the brand so much a few franchises were allowed in the vicinity.

Young boys would try to convince us they weren't checking for us when we walked in. They posted up on walls with their faces to their cell phones, eyeing us from their peripheral. Older people waiting for food their doctors and blood pressure and blood sugar told them to avoid.

If we didn't want fries, we'd head to Popeye's on Euclid and Superior near Superior Elementary for a chicken and biscuit deal. I had to have apple jelly and honey with it. Man! Talk about pure sweetness drizzling all the way down the back of my throat. But our all time favorites were B&M's corn beef sandwich or polish boy, which was a fried polish sausage on a bun served with fries, coleslaw, and barbecue sauce wrapped in foil to trap and marinate the deliciousness. This spot was behind the rapid station. It was our main station, and while most call it a train station we called it a rapid.

If I wanted to kick it with Ketra, or any of my friends, it had to be outside. I wasn't allowed in anyone's house and no one was allowed in mines. There was no point in even asking for a one time allowance. You already knew the answer. No need in playing yourself by asking. Ketra lived by pretty much the same rules. Her family was old school too. She and five siblings that were raised by her grandmother in a two bedroom, one bathroom duplex. Come to think of it, I became an accidental cheerleader when I was eleven because of this chick.

We were hanging out one day when Ketra decided she just had to try out for cheerleading. She was super girly so this was right up her alley. With both of her brothers playing football it seemed natural she would cheer. I couldn't stand Elijah, even fought him a few times. Devon expressed serious issues any time we didn't play with him. It was so aggravating. He was quiet unless he wasn't being involved in everything. Then he made the biggest fuss you'd ever see. He was the third of six children so being left out or alone was uncomfortable for him. Damn. I would never want to be around anyone who didn't want to be around me. I didn't understand him.

Now, somehow Ketra heard tryouts were being held at Forrest Hill Park. She pleaded with me to go up there with her. Finally I caved. I tagged along with Ketra to Forrest Hill Park, taking a basketball to keep me occupied in case the process took a while. So, here I was, in typical tomboy mode, dribbling my heart out, playing around, and waiting for my friend so we could get on with our day. I wasn't where the actual basketball court was, but I was bouncing the ball, speaking to random people passing by. Out of nowhere, a coach named Donna walks up to me. Mind you, I'm in hooping shorts and a shirt. The mole under her right eye was the first thing I noticed about the large brown woman with her brown hair pulled back in a thick ponytail, beating against her back as she approached.

"Would you like to cheer?" She asked, hope shining in her eyes.

I pivoted on my heels. Clearly she was speaking to someone behind me. "Nah. That ain't my thing." This lady was in fact talking to me! Was she blind? I held the ball front and center to underscore my statement. "I don't like that kind of stuff." It was my impression they would want girls who dreamed of being a part of the squad. Not girls like me who had to be begged.

Her angle was me having an amazing voice. Her exact wording was, "I love your voice." She advised my raspy alto carried across the park and caught their attention. I was thrown for a loop. Having a deeper voice as a female was a source of insecurity for me. I had never been complimented on it before. No. I take that back. A few adults said my singing voice reminded them of how Toni Braxton sounded and they felt I had the potential to sing the same. They assumed I sang since they liked my singing voice, I didn't.

As a matter of fact, I had been mistaken for a boy once. I called a friend's house in kindergarten. Her mom answered and advised she couldn't receive calls from boys. It was a gut punch. Is that how they felt when they heard me speak?

Nothing about me said 'cheerleader'. In my mind, cheerleaders sounded like Valley girls. I gave Donna every reason in the world why I couldn't cheer. I hemmed and hawed, but eventually gave in. She should have been a recruiter. For every argument I raised, she had a convincing rebuttal. Donna promised to teach me everything I would need to know. Ketra ended up more excited about me joining than her being accepted; probably because she expected her acceptance. My cheering meant the best friends would have more things to do together. We became part of the East Cleveland Chiefs rocking orange, blue, and white. The team was considered Munny League in that we only competed against city teams, nothing larger.

One of my most memorable cheer moments was taking a team bus to a cheer competition in North Carolina. This was one of those trips where girls shared rooms and created bonding memories. Being best friends, Ketra and I requested to share one. Though we didn't get the grandest lodgings or fanciest dinner, traveling out of town for competitions thrilled us. Most parents packed food so their children had something to eat on the road. Others were given a few dollars to grab a bite during our stops. Always having my own stash, I was good. Aunt Genie gave me some extra, but even if she hadn't, I had enough to eat while we were gone.

Our biggest local rivals were the Sims Raiders. Their cheers were really creative and the crowd loved them, but what I remember the most was the hideous black and white Oxfords with the rubber sole they wore. Hideous. I hated those shoes. We joked them every time we cheered against them.

Ketra, Erica, Jediah and I started feeling ourselves in a major way. They didn't cheer with us, but they had their own things going on. We decided to be a cohesive front by calling ourselves a fake gang, BWA or Bitches With Attitude, wearing pink when we were 'banging'. Admittedly NWA had something to do with the name we chose. We found it dope and relevant.

One other thing Ketra and I shared was an interest in Brandon. He was two years older than me and lived on my block. He was fine as hell. I felt lucky to look at him every day. No people, this is not the same Brandon from 2nd grade. Like anyone my age with a crush, I stayed in the windows, checking the streets for him. If I saw him, I went out, even when I hadn't planned to be outside. I never made a move though. I couldn't. My interest in Brandon was secreted away in the far recesses of my adolescent mind. Ketra had the spot as his girlfriend. Us being besties, girl code went into full effect. There were no hard feelings either. Ketra was a pretty brown girl with long hair. The boys always went for her.

Nissan, Fatboy, and Andre lived in the same duplex, two houses down from me on the corner. Nissan's family lived upstairs and Andre and Fatboy lived downstairs. Andre was born deaf. I don't know if the disability had anything to do with it or not, but his head was unnaturally long. He was a toffee, slender boy of average height. Playing with him made us learn responsibility for one another. We had to make sure he didn't get hit by emergency vehicles flying through the streets because he couldn't hear the sirens. We had to make sure we considered him when playing hide and seek because he would not hear us calling for him if he wandered too far. We even picked up some sign language in order to communicate with him which inspired my two years of ASL in college.

Our penny pinching community shocked us by getting a 'Deaf Child' sign erected on our block. Vehicles paid it as much attention as any other common street sign they blew by. I'm not even sure they understood what they needed to do when driving on a street where a deaf child resided. Not to say people are dumb, just when you don't deal with it in your everyday life you are ignorant of the sensitivities and dangers. The gesture was appropriate and caring. It was the best money spent, not because it worked but because it showed a sense of community. Especially since you couldn't get us to share resources to fund anything.

Fatboy, whom we called Pork Chop to antagonize him, was named Deonte, but no one ever called him that. He was hefty, short, and could never keep up when we ran so he always tried to convince us to play games with little to none of it. Tamara never made it to the status of a best friend. She played with us because she was on the block. I beat the bully out of her, ridding her of the misconception she would be picking on me the way she did everyone else. Once I helped her understand I wasn't the one, we got along just fine. Most people thought she liked girls because she dressed like a boy, but she didn't.

The other girls distanced themselves from her, thinking she like them. If it pissed her off and she fought them, they would think she was behaving like a boy: picking with them out of adoration.

Erica was a newcomer to our block. She had to be trained on how to deal with me. Her issue wasn't bullying. She just didn't treat me the way I wanted to be treated. I learned early that if you let people get away with too much you won't like how you are dealt with more times than not. Then there were others I occasionally hung out with: Elisha and Laquila were a set, then Sharda, Cassandra, and Cece. We had a friend Ricky whose siblings were adopted. You could easily feel like an odd wheel when dealing with siblings because they already have a bond and friendship. You never infiltrate it, you're just a welcome supplement.

The entire gang of us spilled out into the streets when homework was done or after breakfast on the weekends. Rounds of any bounce broke out whenever a ball was struck with a bat and someone caught it on a bounce without it rolling. Our group created a version of football not quite tag or touch. Then there was the normal freeze tag, hide and seek, dino man, and nigga knock. Nigga knock probably got us in the most trouble since we were banging on people's doors and running, which they found very annoying.

If youth weren't in the streets, they could be found at the Martin D. Pores center. It was a safe haven and parents would drop their children off there for a few hours so they could run errands instead of leaving them unsupervised. They also provided free lunch and activities during the summer and weekends.

Even better, many northern urban communities had a block party each year. It was hosted by the community center under the bridge at the top of Elberon. Ketra, Kimberly, Erica, and I formed a dance group when I was 9-years-old. The idea came from hearing people, especially our families, tell us we should start a group after seeing us dance together. Anytime a song came on we were moving to the beat. My generation got pumped hearing Master P's *Bout It, Bout It* and other rap hits of the '90s. And why wouldn't we? We were 'bout it'.

We felt the lyrics applied to our lives. Mia X said it clearly in one of her verses in the song, "Cause in this drama field, fool we ain't takin' no shit'.

At first, the group did drills under the name No Limit Soldiers but later changed to New Edition. Ketra and I split due to bumping heads over leadership. She was replaced by Candace, who later left the group because her mom was so strict. Candace's mom kept her in the house, making it hard for her to practice. I think she felt the music and group were a bad influence. Without Candace we transitioned to hip-hop as the Hot Girls and Ketra came back. Routines were created to Missy's *Hot Boyz*, Project Pat's *Chickenhead*, and TLC's *I'm Good At Being Bad*. We never had uniforms but we tried our best to match. The group agreed on sky blue as our color. I had these sparkling blue pants I paired with a light blue shirt with blue and white Nikes. We also felt we were too fly to perform without our hair professionally done either. The crowds loved us. A few trophies went home with us, but nothing major came of it.

It seemed the entire hood showed up every time to enjoy the performances, barbecue food, and raffles. Raffles meant you won something so everyone loved them. I walked away with a pink Huffy 12-speed one year. Man, I loved winning the bike. However, what I would have loved more was my family seeing me in action. I started noticing my family had no problem supporting my endeavors financially, but still didn't find it necessary to actually show up. It really sucked too because my family would build me up to do something and I felt they should follow through by attending my events.

Part of me wondered if they encouraged me to do things to keep me busy and out of the way. My grandma and granddad were older. They didn't have it in them to run up and down the road behind an active child. My parents couldn't be counted on and I refused to set myself up for disappointment with them. Aunt Genie's way of being supportive was always to throw money and call it a day. Which was all fine, but if I asked her why she didn't fund more important things than my wardrobe, like college, she said I wasn't her child so it wasn't her job to invest in me to that extent. Her advice was for me to be grateful for what I did get.

Hard as it may be to believe, I did spend some time inside of the house. Television held my interest if the right thing was on. This was also hang time with my grandma. My favorite shows were Family Matters, Full House, Ricky Lake, Montel Williams, Geraldo, Sally, Ahh Real Monsters, Rugrats, As The World Turns, Young and The Restless, Bold and The Beautiful, Hey Arnold, and my favorite-Jerry Springer. The soaps had drama, but Jerry! We were so convinced we would witness a live murder if we just kept watching. Some of these beat downs were better than the ones we saw in the hood. It was also a silent hope Jerry would get taken down in the midst of a rumble since he instigated them. He seemed to always jump out of the way right in the nick of time. On days I didn't have drill team or basketball practice I hightailed home to catch my 4 p.m. show.

If the coast was clear, Jamiel allowed me to watch Queer As Folk, Sex In The City, OZ, and other shows my grandma forbade me to view. The programs were full of sexual content, profanity, and violence. I was exposed to enough of this mess in real life without being inundated with it over the airwaves. He didn't mind being my accomplice in these crimes. You have to know which family members would let you get away with what. He taught me to be uncompromising unless absolutely necessary.

Unconventional activities- that was Jamiel too. I only ever told Keisha this, but I even found gay male porn mags in his drawer. It confirmed what the family already suspected. I never judged him or thought twice about it. He was just Jamiel to me.

As school progressed, I started struggling more. One would assume 1991's DeRolf v. State of Ohio reformed education for the entire state, but obviously not. The Ohio Coalition for Equity & Adequacy of School funding filed suit against the state for failing to provide sufficient funding. The case continued through appeals until 1997. While the way Ohio funded school system was deemed unconstitutional the ruling itself wasn't a solution. The problem they were left with was the lack of guidance provided on how to fund programs.

They had the resources but not the knowledge of how to manage them. A complete revamp continues to be a focal point for advocates statewide.

Cleveland's system was unique in its indolence, inability or desire to secure resources and creative curriculum or programs to engage students. Overcoming is an entirely different struggle here. A typical school year consisted of four classes per grade with thirty to forty students crammed into each, clearly far more than one teacher could efficiently handle, or provide individual attention to say the least.

The four classes offered were known to us as honors, almost honors, a step above remedial, and remedial. You are classified and set on course from kindergarten. This prevented a child from being placed in classes where they would benefit from a better curriculum later in their academic life even if they qualified. For example, if you were in almost honors you would be in almost honors classes year after year. There wouldn't be a course title to identify it, you just knew it.

The books, they were far, few, and in shabby condition. If you had one, you vigilantly guarded it. If you were caught slipping with it out of your possession you could kiss it goodbye. Impoverished students yearning to learn picked lockers to scavenge supplies. Most children were provided Xeroxed copies of entire books bound together instead of the real book and had to make due. Can you imagine? Children. From the hood. Given copied pages of textbooks and being expected to keep up with them? They rarely ever kept track of all of the pages.

Those of us fortunate or gifted enough found a dynamic mentor. Ms. Hives changed my life forever. I fought constantly and stayed in trouble or suspended. Surprise, surprise. I was a lot for some teachers; Mrs. Wagner my 4th grade teacher in particular. She spitefully decided my intelligence was of no consequence and that my behavior warranted I get delegated to the remedial classes. This was a common way to deal with students who behaved the way I did.

I struggled immensely in 4th grade under Mrs. Wagner. Not because I was dumb, but like so many other students, my learning style was unique to me and these teachers lacked the patience, time, skills, resources, and often the desire to work with each child in a way that reached them. School started seeming like a tumultuous assembly belt from childhood to adulthood without tools for survival or success.

To find an outlet, besides my sports, I tried out for the choir. I didn't think I would get it. My voice was a major challenge for me. Hilariously, I slid in by the hair on my chinny chin chin because the teacher thought I was sick. The joke was on her because, yep, it was my normal voice. It wasn't girly the way other girls my age sounded. I got accepted, which shocked me, but as soon as she realized how I truly sounded, needless to say, she didn't approve an encore for the next semester. Some of the kids even teased me that semester when they heard me sing, but I never cared. I got to experience choir.

To top off the trauma of 4th grade, a near rape threw me into a downward spiral of anxiety. I was walking home from school, passing a building with a small alleyway. I'd been walking home by myself for years and never thought anything of it. I knew to look out for myself, but I didn't think of him as a threat. So, I'm walking up to the alley and a boy from around the way named Josiah is walking toward me. As I come to the opening of the alleyway Josiah shoves me in.

It took me by surprise to the point I didn't scream immediately. I half thought it was a joke since we knew each other. Boys pushed girls all the time. When I realized it was deeper than that my instinct to fight kicked in. Josiah dragged me to the other side of a dumpster, out of view from the sidewalk. He started digging in my pants, squeezing my chest. No matter how much I swung to knock his head off he just kept dodging me. I remember the nasty feeling of his mouth as it came down on the side of my face in an attempt to kiss me. I turned my head to the side just in time to avoid it landing on my mouth. I thrust my knees into his crotch to get him off of me. I missed my target: his penis. I squirmed and fought but never screamed. I don't know why. Maybe I just wanted to escape him immediately and hadn't thought to bother calling for help.

As Josiah held me down by placing all of his weight on top of me and holding both my wrist above my outstretched body with one hand, he used his other hand to continue trying to find its way further into my panties. Horror, but more than that, fury seized me. This boy had the audacity to feel entitled to do whatever he wanted to me. I swore when I got up I was going to beat him near death. I planned to ensure he'd never think about doing this to another girl. As my promises to avenge myself ran through my head, the weight of his body suddenly lifted off of me.

Josiah's breath audibly rushed out of him as his back hit the wall of the building. I scrambled to my feet and saw my on and off boyfriend Jonathan's fist slam into the side of Josiah's face. The two went at it for a few moments, Josiah clearly losing. Finally Jonathan's blows sent Josiah running toward the street.

Jonathan told me he saw Josiah shove me into the alley from up the block and came to check on me when he noticed we hadn't come back out. He walked me all the way home to make sure Josiah didn't follow me to finish what he started. I had no idea how scared I was until I realized my shaking was making it hard for me to walk. Jonathan kept asking if I was okay. I can't imagine anyone is ever okay after some shit like that. I didn't know what to make of the whole situation. Josiah never attempted to take my clothes off. Was he playing and just took it too far or was his real intention to rape me? I never found out. I never asked. Josiah kept his distance from me and I did the same. If he had come near me again, I would have kept my promise to myself as a precaution.

When Mrs. Wagner made this decision to sabotage my education, I was placed in Ms. Hives class for 5th grade. She was the type of teacher who brought clothes and supplies to school for disadvantaged students so they could wash

> **AS JOSIAH HELD ME DOWN BY PLACING ALL OF HIS WEIGHT ON TOP OF ME AND HOLDING BOTH MY WRIST ABOVE MY OUTSTRETCHED BODY WITH ONE HAND, HE USED HIS OTHER HAND TO CONTINUE TRYING TO FIND ITS WAY FURTHER INTO MY PANTIES.**

and change at school. It would be three or five hours after school dismissed before she left, devoting extra time teaching students how to read. Ms. Hives was so valuable to the community she was the only teacher parents allowed to chastise their children because they knew her intentions were good.

I don't say this to insinuate there were no other teachers with an interest in the well-being of the students. Several existed. They understood what home life was for many of us. Some even came up in our same neighborhoods and were a product of our educational system. Their hope was to pump as much as they could into us to push us through whatever we were facing outside of class.

In some sense, teachers were an extension of parents. They nurtured us, supported us, taught us, reprimanded us, and guided us on our academic journey. Teachers who had been doing the job long enough saw through the crap we gave them and noticed our potential. They weren't always successful in cultivating talents, but thankfully it didn't stop them and plenty of us made something of ourselves. I don't know about everywhere else, but in East Cleveland, you weren't finding too many parents helping their children with homework after school or prepping for test over the weekend. Almost all the responsibility for educating children fell on the teachers.

Not only did Ms. Hives show interest in me during the school year, but she made sure I was good when school was out. Each summer she hired me the first two and last two weeks of summer to clean up and organize the classrooms. My labor earned one hundred dollars per day and all my meals for the day. If other teachers wanted my help when they saw what I was doing for her, she made them pay me. She refused to let them take advantage of me.

My intellect made my presence in Ms. Hives class a mystery. I believe that's why she took such an interest in me. I didn't belong there. One of these things was not like the others. To top it off, my test scores were the highest in the state of Ohio that year. Despite my test scores, the procedure was for me to enter 6th grade in remedial classes. Ms. Hives wasn't having it. She placed me in the honors class, instructing the teacher to come to her if she had any issues out of me. She wanted to be the one to deal with me. In her mind, no one else knew how to get through to me. With her diligence and devotion to helping students willing to be helped, I received the best education this comparatively subpar system had to offer.

In addition to this, she enrolled me in Mrs. Biggerstaff's anger management course. I attended the class one hour per day. What would the point of it all be if my attitude and behavior prevented my progress? I realize she took the full picture into account by providing all the resources she could find to support me.

By 6th grade, I started struggling with boredom having completed all of my work early. Mind you, I'm in honors classes. To remedy this, I began a newspaper committee. Surprisingly, it met with success. The paper staffed a few students and the library granted us special permission to use the computers. Vice Principal Dr. Johnson facilitated our committee, oversaw the editing, and ensured publications were printed and delivered timely. I felt extreme pride. The newspaper was a major contribution to my school and it proved the faculty wrong regarding their prejudiced opinions of me based on my prior behavior.

Had Ms. Hives not been my advocate, I would not have been in the honors classes I deserved to be in during middle school. Little did I know it would be those classes which allowed me to enter CAPS once I advanced to 7th grade. Enrollment in honors courses was a requirement or you wouldn't qualify. Ms. Hives boasted about my academic prowess and ability to behave when given the opportunity to engage in quality education. She was the one who provided my letter of recommendation. No other teacher would have written anything to encourage my entry into the program.

For participants, CAPS provided one Saturday class a month for additional science education which included dissecting animals and hands-on chemical reactions. I only remember cutting open a frog and a squid, nothing large. We hoped for pigs, sharks, and rodents like we heard other schools. Our CAPS didn't have the resources for it. This was not available to students within the standard curriculum and the course was restricted to a maximum of twenty students, making it highly competitive. In short, in order to receive a viable education you needed an advocate. Meaning, out of 120-160 students, you had to shine bright to not be overlooked. While we felt advanced being accepted into the course, in reality, it was a standard course in most school systems.

I couldn't just release her out of my life once she was no longer my teacher. She meant too much to me. It was her who helped me get my first apartment at seventeen so I could get custody of my baby sister when I turned eighteen. Let's put a pin in that for now. I promoted her from her prior post as my teacher to my godmother. Over the years, she continued to help me map my path to success.

The only struggle I had attending CAPS was being tired from my Friday nights. Fridays were for Roller Dome. It was the spot to be EVERY Friday without fail. This was the only time many of us were able to socialize with peers outside of our community. Guys lived for the opportunity to check out a fresh selection of girls, and girls enjoyed escaping the exhausted, limited options from their schools or neighborhoods. You got bored being around the same people you grew up with. It was exciting to switch it up and experience someone new. As you can imagine, we dressed to impress. It rivaled dressing on the first day of school. If you had some money, you probably brought a new outfit. You definitely got your hair done. Girls were in skirts or short shorts with their legs greased up or tight pants. Boys wore whatever jewelry they could scrounge up and too much of their dad's cologne.

The best part was the segments for couples, backward, or group skate. People showed their asses at the rink. You saw tricks, people won prizes for competitions, and you definitely witnessed them bite the dust when a stunt didn't go as planned. Popularity belonged to the members of the skate crews. We treated them like stars of a major sports team. Many even had favorites; definitely crushes.

The atmosphere was electric. Your heart felt like it beat to the music when you stepped inside. Disco balls sent the most beautiful light show dancing across the walls and ceilings. Every time the groups jumped, their skates hitting the floor in unison sent shock waves you could feel vibrating through the floor. The trip to Euclid's Lakeshore area for the rink was worth every moment.

The rink had a few games for those who loved the environment, but didn't want to skate. A few snacks could be purchased, nachos being my favorite. I couldn't imagine not having memories from the Roller Dome. Every childhood should have experiences akin to it. Then, to our dismay, our good thing came to an end. We were from the hood after all. Eventually, fights began breaking out over the slightest infraction or misunderstanding. Euclid police peppersprayed both offender and non-offenders alike. Ketra and I had to abandon our favorite spot as a result of the wild outbreaks.

Right before we abandoned the rink, I wound up meeting a dude. Dominic, or Nick as we called him, asked me to be his girl after meeting me there. Guess after watching me show off the way I did I caught his attention. Since my bestie Ketra was with me most of the time, she and his cousin De'erick wound up dating. It was fun. Best friends and cousins. It certainly made things convenient. Our parents expected Ketra and I to be together, which made it easy for us to see our boyfriends without them knowing.

Dominic Morgan stood 5'8 and had a smile that could replace the sun. Our normal meet up spot was the Roller Dome, but every blue moon his mom, Cynthia, allowed me to come over to the house on Waterloo and Lakeshore. It wasn't worth it, although we liked seeing each other. His mom kept her hawk-like gaze on us. Nothing, and I mean nothing, was going down on her watch. I'm not going to lie, I wanted to touch and kiss so she was in the way. Cynthia tried to make me feel comfortable, but she wanted it known we couldn't do anything. She invited me over to see the Bernard-Hopkins fight in an attempt to show she accepted me. We ate the lasagna she made for the event. Her boyfriend was there and I guess she thought it would be cute for her son to have a date as well. I couldn't have been more stoked. Now we had two adults monitoring our every move.

The only other time I can remember being at their house was his birthday. It was an old-fashioned house party; the kind where parents put all the children in the basement to get them out of the way and confine them at the same time. She got him a deejay and all of the boys in attendance did what they always do: lined the walls and let the girls bounce and grind their butts against their pelvises. We danced until one of us needed a break, then we'd dash over to the folding table covered with a table cloth and lined with a skirt. The table held a pan of spaghetti, a pan of fried chicken, sodas, paper plates, plastic cups, plastic cutlery, and his cake. I don't know why all parties had chicken and spaghetti, but in Cleveland, those were party must-haves.

Beyond that, we met at De'erick's on 55th and Superior, right behind the McDonald's and Marathon, whenever he wasn't on punishment. This was the only place Cynthia allowed him to go. Since they were family, in her mind, his being there was the same as him being at home. She communicated his restrictions and curfew directly with De'erick's mom, and grandmother living above them in their duplex, to remove any margin of error on his part.

As anyone could guess, my puppy love with Nick dissipated after four months because his mom was too strict for us to grow anything real. Not that a 'real' relationship was possible at our age, but throughout the years we could have developed into more as we matured. His freedom was restricted, making my access to him extremely limited. And being a teenage boy, his testosterone kept him on punishment. I started realizing I would never get to really spend time with him. The only time we could speak if we weren't in person was if he snuck phone calls since he was always on punishment, or if he used De'erick's phone. It was crazy. I felt like I was dating a boy in juvie or a boy's home. And forget when he was suspended from school, which was often, it was like he ceased to exist. I was too young to deal with this much restriction. He had me feeling like I was the one on punishment.

Ketra and De'erick also broke up eventually. Weirdly enough, he and I became long-term best friends. His family treated me like I was one of their own. It felt like a see-saw, to be honest. The closer I got to De'erick, the further into the background Ketra faded. I never meant for it to happen. De'erick was just such a good friend and Ketra didn't want to be around when he was, which was often. Life is funny that way. He attended my 8th grade graduation and every other major milestone in support of my achievements until his death in 2012, right before his birthday.

My heart cracked when De'erick joined the multitude of stereotypes buried young in urban America. Attracted to trouble and the streets, he became heavily involved with drug trafficking in his neighborhood. You most often caught a glimpse of him behind the same McDonald's or Marathon gas station off of 55th Nick would have me meet him at. There weren't many other opportunities for our youth with the education they were provided and the jobs being offered. If they lacked the ability to relocate, they stuck to what they knew.

Rumor had it he became too big and one of the people closest to him killed him out of jealousy. It was a common occurrence. Envy is a terrible thing. I mourned him deeply. Waves of pain and sadness swept over me constantly when I first got the news. I lived in Hawaii when it happened so I missed the funeral. I kept thinking of how he lost his father to the streets during his childhood only to leave his two sons behind in the same manner with his long-term girlfriend Janiqua. I respected her. Regardless of their differences, they had their own on and off love affair, they co-parented very well. They loved their children and he did what it took to give them the world, legal or not. He was one of the kindest people I knew. If I ever needed anything and

> **MY HEART CRACKED WHEN DE'ERICK JOINED THE MULTITUDE OF STEREOTYPES BURIED YOUNG IN URBAN AMERICA. ATTRACTED TO TROUBLE AND THE STREETS, HE BECAME HEAVILY INVOLVED WITH DRUG TRAFFICKING IN HIS NEIGHBORHOOD.**

he found out, he did whatever it took to help me out. Whenever I wanted to smoke or sell some weed, but couldn't find any, he hooked me up. His streams of income were unlawful, but his heart was good.

I hated hearing people judge him for being in the streets. I reminded them every chance I got about the high level of corruption and illegal activity in politics and corporate America. Everyone looks out for themselves. They just get in where they fit in to do it best. I later found out his younger brother started following in his footsteps. Instead of viewing his brother's demise as a lesson he saw him as a role model. Life is perspective.

Speaking of the streets, my dad was still around, here and there. He would stop by and catch up with me, making sure I was alright. You could tell he was proud I hadn't turned out to be a soft girl. I knew how to take care of myself, and for a father, that's important. It's one of the first things parents of any species instill in their offspring: learning to survive in the wild. This visit happened on a really cool day. My dad was sitting on the front porch alone with a beer. I followed him out because I didn't see him a lot so, why not. We talked about nothing in particular while trying to catch up on everything since our last visit. A light breeze blew across the porch every couple of minutes. The kind of slow, lingering, refreshing breeze which brings crisp oxygen into your lungs and washes off and out of you like a detox.

Every time my dad absent-mindedly lifted his can to his lips for a sip, my eyes were drawn to it. Beads of moisture clung to it from being in the fridge and his lips parted slightly each time to allow the liquid entry. I must have been staring hard as hell because he paused mid-swig and turned to me.

"Dang girl." He chuckled. "You all down my throat. You want some or something?"

The offer took me by surprise. *Did I?* He shoved the can in my face. He said he couldn't finish it in peace without me taking a sip since I was watching him so hard. I took the cold can in my adolescent hand and lifted it up to my face. Building myself up for my first taste of beer, I sniffed it. Finally, I tilted my head back and took a gulp. I didn't know what to expect, but this wasn't it. The way adults guzzled beer I figured it tasted like a better form of soda. I couldn't have been more wrong. The bitter, harsh taste stayed on my tongue longer than desired. I was done with it, for now.

I headed inside to replace the taste in my mouth. My favorite food was watermelon. It was sweet and juicy. Grandma kept some in the fridge for me when they were in season. My dad said I would eat it until I threw up I loved it so much. I searched the shelves for what was left from our last trip to Finast. Nothing. Someone must have eaten it. Everyone knew it was my favorite food, but if it was in the house it was for the house.

I decided to go for my favorite dessert: banana pudding. My dad brought some with him and placed it in the fridge for me. He normally did this when he came to see me. Now this, they would leave alone. I took the container out and scooped a small bit into a bowl. The indulgence had to be quick. If my grandma caught me, I would have to hear the 'sweets before dinner' talk. I wasn't about to explain to her that I simply needed to get the taste of beer out of my mouth.

Entering my teens, I felt ruled by the same thing most teens lived for; their social life. Man, I remember taking trips out to Wickliffe, where the only dollar movie in the area was located. On Sunday's movies were only fifty cents. This brought everyone out. The only down side was every concession stand was shut down except the front on discount day and even though the movies were discounted, the snacks weren't. It was set up for you to get your snacks up front, then you would head down the hall to your theater, passing the mini concession stations that were opened on regularly priced days. I don't know what made us think of it, but it dawned on Keisha and me that boxes full of candy and perishables should be stashed behind the stands. We decided either she or I would play the role of lookout while the other jumped over the counter to raid it for as much as we could. Our favorite items were licorice or whoppers. Ironically, to this day I can't stand the taste or smell of either because we engorged ourselves with them. The very sight of watching others eat them makes me cringe. I came to respect the motto, 'everything in moderation'.

> **I TOOK THE COLD CAN IN MY ADOLESCENT HAND AND LIFTED IT UP TO MY FACE. BUILDING MYSELF UP FOR MY FIRST TASTE OF BEER, I SNIFFED IT.**

We ended up with so many boxes of candy, selling them door to door in Parkside Gardens became lucrative. If we ran out, we would go to every CVS in our vicinity to steal mini candy bars. Yeah, steal. We were trying to make money, not spend it. Then we would knock on every door in the apartment complex. I don't know why, but Deedee and I were with them for an extended amount of time, so I believe we were living with them again. We made so much money selling candy door to door. Candy was a hit for us because children are always buying it and we were coming to them so they didn't have to go out for it. I guess we were something like the complex candy ladies.

My aunt Lawanda had an older male friend, Cliff, who stayed in an apartment across the hall from her. She'd take us over to his apartment to watch T.V. while she was with him. We couldn't wait for them to go to sleep. That's when we could watch X-rated scenes and movies. One of them even had Janet Jackson or Halle Berry in them. There were a lot of mischievous things we found ourselves doing. This included being on the Rave, a popular chat line back in the day. We were developing and our curiosity was as well.

A chat line worked exactly how the name suggests. You called into the chat line number and answered questions to get you directed to the line you wanted to be on. It would ask if you were a male or female and if you were interested in males or females. Come to think of it, it was the phone version of an online dating site. We would hear a person's tagline and select to speak with them or skip them, moving you on to the next. I never had time to do any picking because I was always getting selected. I had some smooth, unbothered line like, "Yeah, I'm a chill chick just up here to see what's going on." If you really enjoyed speaking to someone you would give them your number or even meet with them in person. I did it a few times. That was a major way we found new people to kick it with back then.

After a while, Keisha wound up at her grandmother's house in Strongsville on the west side during the weekends. She had a nice apartment in the suburbs on Ohio's west side where Keisha enjoyed a temporary escape from hood shenanigans; which she was often a part of. We were always living between different family residences. Her grandmother raised her mostly, leaving me alone with my mother and aunt at the apartment on the weekends in her absence. Life must have been good for her over there because every time she came back her hair was in a new style, particularly boxed or crochet braids.

During one of the periods they were forced to stay with us at Ruth's house, Keisha earned an epic ass whipping. In all honesty, I deserved one too. I'm not sure why I was spared. We managed to rack up a few hundred dollars in phone bills by calling the sex hotline number we saw streaming across the T.V. screen late at night. These calls were made from either my grandma's house or Cliff's house in the wee hours of the morning. Keisha's mom didn't have a phone for us to use or we would have made calls from there too. They wound up connecting the dots and realizing it was us because we were the common denominators at the locations during those hours. They had been commiserating back and forth about these astronomical telephone bills when it finally hit them. They were pissed.

"What the hell y'all calling these sex numbers for?" Ruth demanded.

"We don't know." I said. I knew damn well why we called. We wanted to know what was being said up there. "We saw the number and wanted to know what it was."

"Y'all knew what it was. You saw the commercial." Aunt Lawanda said. "You know what you were seeing on the commercial, right?"

There was no need to continue answering questions. It was self-incrimination. We just took the punishment. Well, Keisha did.

When I wasn't getting into shit with Keisha, I was getting into shit with Ketra. She was my go-to in the streets. Normally, I was ahead of the curve on things when it came to our social lives, but she pulled forward on me with the fashion. Ketra was rocking Coach purses, belts, and shoes of all colors and styles. The chick appeared to be balling. Coach was the designer of the day in the hood. You wore if you could afford it to avoid looking whack. I pleaded with Jamiel and Genie to get me a few items. Months of me begging went by while this chick was popping up with shade after shade, color and style of Coach this and Coach that. Six months and a few thoughts of boosting later, Jamiel caved. I'm glad he did because it would not have been long before I headed to the mall at the risk of getting caught and apprehended. He got his 11-year-old niece a twelve-hundred-dollar black Coach 'pockabook', as my grandma would say.

I felt like I was on a whole other level. If you could have seen me, you would have told me to slow my roll. I decided to give it a few months before I asked for another piece. It's a good thing I did. The truth came out. Here I was begging, my hard-working family to frivolously spend funds for designer items on an 11-year-old who should have been more focused on being a child and learning, when I found out Ketra's Coach apparel was hot off of the Muslims in bow ties on Euclid and Superior. Knock offs passing for originals. I felt played and foolish for jocking her the way I had. I couldn't allow someone else to be more spoiled than I was, so I pressed my family. It proved just how spoiled I was. To this day, I couldn't care less what someone else has because you never knew how they obtained it or if it was even theirs. Authenticity not only mattered with possessions to me, but with the person.

THEY ALL COME CRASHING DOWN

The worst thing I could never have imagined in my youth occurred. Cancer slithered its way into my granddad's cells and ravaged him. I was 11-years-old when he was diagnosed and 11-years-old when we surrendered his body to the grave. It was one of the hardest periods of my life. It snatched him from us before we got a chance to wrap our minds around it all. I learned at a very tender age how quiet and subtle this disease was. By the time the symptoms manifested, it had already done what it came to do. Losing a part of your foundation interrupts the entire structure. Our family had to recalibrate. I had to deal with the death of a loved one for the first time. This wasn't one of my dogs I lost; this was one of the lead men in my life.

Sadness hung over our days like a cloud of impending doom. I had no idea what cancer was back then. I understood it was a disease, but the absolute savage beast of it was unknown to me. As soon as my granddad was diagnosed a hospice bed arrived to replace the joined twin sets. He never got better. I watched helplessly and hopelessly as my best friend faded away. And to our amazement, he only remembered one person: me.

If you have never experienced the misery of losing a loved one to cancer, let me explain. As death creeps closer they fall victim to delirium. They can recall very few people no matter how important you are to them or how long they've known you. No one can tell for certain why they remember who they do. He didn't remember any of his four children. He couldn't place the love of his life since they were eighteen and the mother of his children. But me, me he knew and called out for.

> **CANCER SLITHERED ITS WAY INTO MY GRANDDAD'S CELLS AND RAVAGED HIM. I WAS 11-YEARS-OLD WHEN HE WAS DIAGNOSED AND 11-YEARS-OLD WHEN WE SURRENDERED HIS BODY TO THE GRAVE. IT WAS ONE OF THE HARDEST PERIODS OF MY LIFE. IT SNATCHED HIM FROM US BEFORE WE GOT A CHANCE TO WRAP OUR MINDS AROUND IT ALL.**

Watching my grandparents age, knowing they would pass eventually, and how their energy and bodies were changing was hard enough. Yet, witnessing the unraveling of this active, social pillar was shattering. He frequented the streets, hanging with friends, and running here or there. It all ended abruptly. His features became sunken and this tower of a man withered away before my eyes. A few weeks later, he was on a respirator. Every time I blinked he was in a more diminished state.

Shortly after, Ketra and I were playing hide-and-seek outside when my aunt Genie asked if I wanted to visit my granddad in the hospice. He had been removed from the home. I didn't. Not because I didn't want to see him. I just didn't want to see him like that. It scared me. The importance of relishing each moment and how precious each opportunity to see him had been lost to me. I was just too young to understand. My family didn't force the visits on me either. They knew how much pain it caused me. We lost him around midnight of the same day. Three months. From diagnosis to the grave was a ferocious, swift three months. Not going to see him ranks amongst the top regrets I carry with me today.

True to form, my aunt and grandmother made sure he was dapper when laid to rest. We buried him at either Greens Lakeview or Highlands. I can't remember. I seriously believe I suppressed a lot of his passing because of the pain. Even now, in my thirties, if his memory finds its way to the surface of my consciousness, I'm forced to ask, "Why did you have to leave me?" I can't begin to imagine the memories we would have stored up or the relationship he would have with my children. I would love to still have him.

After losing her husband, my grandma felt she gained a guardian angel. It seemed he warned her every time something bad loomed on the horizon. She told us he often showed up to visit her, even when we moved houses. We believed her. Her speech was matter-of-fact when she described his appearances. And it never unsettled her. Instead, a blanket of comfort and peace would fall over her. It probably felt therapeutic. She had to miss him more than we could ever imagine. They weren't just co-parents, lovers, spouses, cohabitants-they were yin and yang, best friends.

He had been in all of our lives from birth. We never accepted his complete absence. In fact, we all believe he is still actively supporting and counseling us from above. So much love doesn't just die. His spirit still guides our family.

Ruth deteriorated in the years to follow. Her knee had to be replaced and she failed to adhere to scheduled physical therapy for proper healing. This was another difficult time for me. I just lost my granddad and here she was not taking care of herself. She lost the ability to walk the last ten years of her life and her mental faculties diminished. She started repeating herself and forgetting things with increasing frequency. It was odd to us because she would know certain things without a problem but others would escape her. We didn't trust her to be alone for her own safety. My grandma was no longer the independent, matriarch of the family.

Her diminishing state didn't discourage me from running to her when I needed her though. I knew I couldn't rely on her to jump up and do for me as she had in past years, but the moment I was sick or hurt, I made a beeline for her house. I couldn't help it. She was still my grandma. Something about her spirit caused me to need to lay up under her for peace and healing. I got it every time. Maybe it was ingrained in me since she was my nurturer and caregiver all my life. I gravitated to her when my spirit, body, or mind was off. She was my entire sanctuary.

As if my life wasn't experiencing enough turbulence, things at school took a turn. They let things get pretty abysmal before making any effort to keep us safe, but at last, the time had come. Kirk middle was infested with mold and the foundations and infrastructure were old and unmaintained it was crumbling around us. The school was a lawsuit waiting to happen. We were constantly being told areas were no longer accessible or classes had to be held in a different room because it wasn't safe to use the original class.

Finally, during my 8th grade year, Shaw High became our new home. The decision was made to tear Kirk down. Shaw offered us their basement, where we finished the year like academic refugees. We didn't have our own and we felt it. There was excitement being in a new environment, and around high school students at that. We even started tripping, trying to pick up on their social culture and language.

The honors students got sent to Mayfair Elementary, so we lost the ability to spend time with our friends in those classes during the school day. We only had the honors students at Mayfair. Unfortunately, I wasn't at Mayfair long. Me being me, I couldn't stay out of trouble no matter what opportunities I received. I beat the crap out of this girl for having me messed up in the game. She thought she could run her mouth without getting popped in it. If my name came out of your mouth wrong, my fist went in.

Losing my place in the honors program hurt me academically, but I was too busy enjoying being around the high school students to care. The fights were epic. I had never seen razor blades gliding through air in a rush to slice skin. Watching the guys too old and dumb to still be in high school, checking out girls was a pastime. They just posted up against the walls, booty watching, and 'yo shorty'ing, waiting for the schools to age them out of the system.

Shaw High sat across the street from the Sunoco on Euclid. I stopped by for chips and soda before every basketball game I got the chance to attend. I loved the sport, being a power forward myself, and never took for granted seeing the older students play. I never rode the bench and loved cheering on other players who were fierce in their positions. I was known for my defense and even picked up tips watching others, making me even better.

Then there was the Shaw High band! This is what brought the crowds. They had the baddest band and high steppers. Every year Shaw hosted a Battle of the Bands and blew the house down. No one compared. Videos of them would get posted everywhere. I still check them out on YouTube when I feel nostalgic. They had to fundraise for traveling to competitions and uniforms, but their talent and support kept them on top. Mr. Wilson even got them all the way to China one year. China!

TOLEDO

As summer break approached, plans were made for me to spend time in Toledo with my dad. He and his girlfriend Fran exchanged Cleveland for the change of scenery two hours away. I didn't know anyone in Toledo, never been. I told my dad I didn't want to spend an entire summer somewhere I knew nothing about without anyone I knew. He didn't count. He wouldn't be spending all of his time with me. The compromise was that I could bring one friend. Immediately I knew who would be spending the summer with me in Toledo. My ace, Ketra. Hood parents jump at opportunities to get a break from their children, and this was for an entire summer too. Ketra's mom was packing her stuff before we finished asking if she could go. Especially because she thought Ketra would be in good hands.

My dad drove down in one of those old school conversion vans with a bed in the back. It was a quick turnaround. They picked us up and we got on the road within an hour. Fran worked at a meat deli where she couldn't miss work, but didn't want to let my dad take the trip alone either. This made sense because he didn't have a license so if he got stopped for any reason a licensed driver needed to be present.

The van got us safely to Toledo before I knew it. Ketra and I talked and laughed and joked so much on the way. We were excited to be together somewhere neither of us had been before. We imagined how this new city would be and thought of things to do when we got there: exploring, running things, hustling, and making friends. We didn't even notice when we turned onto Forrest St. Immediately my dad started laying down the rules. A man stayed in the house with them. We weren't to get in his way or bother him. When we washed our clothes, we were to hang them outside on the clothesline to dry. The backyard would take on a whole new look for me which would make it unbearable to be in.

"It's just a damn dog." He barked at his daughter, the animal lover. "They know better and if I had let him get away with it the others would think it was okay." I never accepted this as an excuse. Extreme violence couldn't be seen as the only remedy towards animals.

A few weeks in I remembered just how aggressive my father could be. He had three dogs that he mistreated. Now, an animal's nature is its nature. You can train them and they can love you, but they are still animals. So, my dad was being his aggressive self and tripping, beating on one dog for no reason. The other two dogs had been confused about what they should do and alternated between barking and cowering. Then what happens? The dog bites him. Why he was surprised or upset was beyond me because I was expecting it. The sad part followed. Unable to see the part he played in this incident, he rushes into the house, gets his gun and returns outside to shoot the dog in the head. The two other dogs yelp and retreat. My heart sank. I watched him drag the corpse to the far corner of the yard and bury him in a corner, under the fearful gaze of the remaining two. I hated the backyard after that. Any time I had to go out there I sensed the dog's body and thought of how it was decomposing.

The rest of the summer went much the same. I regretted going. Not only did we have to deal with my dad's aggression, we had to deal with Fran's non-cooking self. Her food was horrible, but the two of them insisted we eat her food. Here is the nail in the coffin. Fran decided to make spaghetti. Now, there are foods you leave alone if you don't know how to make; spaghetti is definitely one. Some like it spicy, some add sugar. You have to choose between thin or thicker noodles, making it meaty or saucier-the variations go on and on. I came from a house where good tasting food was always on the table so nasty food was a no-go for me. Fran's rendition of spaghetti was bland. I couldn't even force it down. Ketra fared better than I. Guess she was used to eating nasty shit.

> **MY HEART SANK. I WATCHED HIM DRAG THE CORPSE TO THE FAR CORNER OF THE YARD AND BURY HIM IN A CORNER, UNDER THE FEARFUL GAZE OF THE REMAINING TWO. I HATED THE BACKYARD AFTER THAT.**

Lucky for me, my dad was at his friend's house a few doors down. I contemplated feeding Fran's spaghetti to the trash, but realized my father could see it. His rule was you didn't leave the table until you ate everything on your plate. No wasting food. He didn't care if you sat at the table until the next morning and he meant it. I couldn't pass this mess over to the dogs for two reasons. First, it would have been animal cruelty. Second, if they didn't like it, which I knew they wouldn't, it would remain as evidence. That would have been a whole other issue, feeding 'human' food to dogs. I would have been deemed ungrateful and more.

Finally, my eyes found my salvation, the sink. His kitchen sink didn't have a fully opened drain garbage disposal. His drain had the holes in it, forcing you to only pour liquid down or you'd have to clean anything left that was too big to go down the five holes. In a rush to dispose of this disgusting meal, I emptied the plate in the sink while Ketra played lookout, rinsed the plate off and never looked back. I should have. Evidence wound itself around the drain openings.

Ketra and I were in the attic, where we roomed, conspiring about some leisure activities we could conjure up to occupy our time, when we heard Fran hollering for my dad up the street. Nosey, we hurried down. This chick threw a full-blown tantrum about me not eating all her nasty ass spaghetti. My dad ran down the street to see what his crying girlfriend was upset about. As soon as his foot landed inside of the house he caught sight of me and commenced to beating me with his hand. I guess he didn't have it in him to find a belt first. I had to get it right then and there.

Devastation made my heart swell to the point of bursting. Not only had he spanked me in front of Ketra, he spanked me period! Between my granddad and my dogs, no one really got an opportunity to whip on me. When it did happen, I always felt a slight sense of betrayal, even if I knew I deserved it. But this time I didn't. My mind could not wrap itself around getting in trouble for not eating food I couldn't digest.

Although he couldn't whip Ketra, since she wasn't his child, the expectation was for her to abide by the same rules which had been so clearly and forcefully laid out for me. And she did. Ketra ate every nasty thing put in front of her in the name of a meal.

His controlling behavior ruined my entire summer. We weren't allowed to eat outside of the house. Not even if the food was free. We had to turn it down. That foolishness was unheard of in the hood. Let someone be giving away free McDonald's, snacks, anything; your parents told you to go get it! It was one less thing they had to spend money on for the day.

To get out of the house and away from him and Fran the snitch, we found anything and everything to do outside. This honestly wasn't hard. We did this back home. Everything we did was outside. Ketra and I spent some time at the library because they had programs for children during summer vacation. They also had incentives for children to engage in reading programs. One day they gave out Taco Bell. When he found out I had accepted the free food he cursed me ten ways to Sunday. I didn't get beat, but it felt as if I had.

And junk food? Forget about it. It might as well have been arsenic. I picked up a game called pokeno and made money off of it to sneak snacks. I had been eating junk food my whole life. One summer with my dad wasn't going to change that. You don't just eradicate sweets from a child's diet and expect them to go along with it. He was super bugging. Sugar, like crack, is addictive. I was not about to go through withdrawal.

Aside from candy, my day to day was missing one other major component: a boy. The son of a couple my dad hung out with caught my attention that summer. They stayed around the corner, but I never tried to speak to him in front of my dad. He didn't try either. We were both too smart to give Herc ammunition. He went on with his boys, and I talked to Ketra as if he wasn't a few feet away. It wasn't until we noticed each other on the basketball court of the Douglas Center, the neighborhood's community center, that we took advantage of the opportunity to introduce ourselves. Ketra and I would cross the alley behind my father's house to get there. The center was right on the other side. We played indoor and outdoor basketball often for fun. The sport had always felt so therapeutic to me. Bouncing a ball, hearing it pound on the court or pavement, lifting off to make a jump shot, all of it freed my mind and put my body at ease. It sounds weird, I know. Being active putting a body at ease, but it did.

The boy's name was Joe or something with a 'J', I can't remember. A girl who balled the way I could always impressed the guys, once they got over the shock and hit to their ego. The fact he enjoyed playing ball with me was pretty cool so we hung out frequently while I was there. We didn't consider ourselves boyfriend and girlfriend per se, but I was the girl who had his attention. Ketra didn't speak to any boys in particular while we were there, so us not having a title was fine by me because we were more of a trio than her being a third wheel.

Joe stole a silver freestyle bike with gold pegs and gave it to me so I could get around. I left it with him when it was time for me to leave. There was no need for me to take it. I don't know where he got it from. Never asked. I didn't care. I thought it was sweet and kept it moving. He was the one who taught me how to play pokeno with dimes and I was so good I made about five dollars a game which was spent getting my sugar fix. Even my dad's roommate took pity on me and snuck me a few bucks behind his back for my store runs. It was crazy. But I remember being told to stay out of his roommate's way so I was super careful not to get caught speaking to him. What I never did again was let the 'informant' catch anything my dad wouldn't approve of.

Summer neared its end and we were scheduled to return home in two weeks. I learned a lot more about my dad being alone with him, without the intervention of my great-grandparents. The unfortunate thing, the lessons weren't over. Fran had put a sour taste in my mouth from early on, but I realized I didn't understand where she was coming from. Fear. It was fear of my abusive, controlling, aggressive father with his unrealistic expectations that shaped her behavior.

I don't know what got into her, but out of nowhere, Fran was overcome with a desire to treat us to pizza. Maybe it was the guilt of knowing two children had come to their home at their requests without receiving the summer experience we anticipated. Who knows. She told us when she got paid we would get the pizza. You can't imagine the glee two deprived preteens felt after being denied fast food for weeks. We salivated at the mere thought of it while we waited. The day we were to get our treat we rode with our dad to pick her up from work.

Let me hit you with this ugly fact. The car was Fran's, but she wasn't allowed to drive it. Yep. My dad never let his women drive, although the cars were theirs. Despite the fact he couldn't keep his license, didn't even have it at this time, his women acquiesced to his rule that he would be the only one driving their vehicles. They were dumb as hell. I could never. Anyway, he drove to get her and as soon as she got in the car we exploded with how happy we were about the pizza.

"Pizza?" My dad asked, puzzled.

"Yeah." We exclaimed. "Fran promised us pizza."

"Oh yeah?" He asked under his breath.

Fran never spoke. We stared back and forth between the two from the rear seat. Fran stared out the side window the entire ride. It later occurred to me that she probably wished she could jump out of the car and run. Run and keep running. The vehicle made its way to a house that looked, unfortunately, more like my dad's house than a pizza place. Our hearts sank. Youth encouraged us to hope against our experiences that summer. We should have known Fran's promise of pizza was too good to be true. Suddenly, shock snatched us out of our stupor. My dad yanked Fran out of her seat and started dragging her into the house. Once inside, he stripped her as he pulled her along the floor to their room.

Her panicked, frightened pleas filled the house. "Michael, please!" She begged. "No Michael. No!!!"

By the time he closed the door, there was a trail of clothes leading to the muffled cries. He beat her down. I would have never thought pizza was worth beating a grown woman over. Then again, it wasn't the pizza. It was submission and obedience. Fran knew how he felt about junk food and she had offered it under his roof. Now I understood why she thought it best to tell on me for throwing away my spaghetti. Better me than her I guess. He would have held her accountable if he found out. He expected her to watch us while she was in the house during his absence.

Ketra and I stood in the middle of the hall, paralyzed. I wondered if people outside could hear Fran. I was sure someone would come knocking at the door to save her at any moment. Maybe even the police. Then I realized his roommate was home. Why hadn't he come down to help Fran? What if this was a common occurrence and he knew to mind his business?

Sadly, Fran was no stranger to my father's physical assaults. Not only had my father negatively impacted her body with his beatings, he poisoned it with the introduction to drugs. I don't know why he insisted his women partake? Control? Manipulation? Common interests? Furthermore, why any grown woman would succumb to demands to enter an addiction they knew to be harmful after a life of not indulging was even harder to understand. Fran was simply just another nice woman who fell for my dad's web of charm and got stuck.

Our Toledo nightmare was cut short and we returned to Cleveland. Ketra and I never really talked about that summer. It was such a waste of youth and sun and days without school work. Later, when I visited Cleveland as an adult, I

> **HE BEAT HER DOWN. I WOULD HAVE NEVER THOUGHT PIZZA WAS WORTH BEATING A GROWN WOMAN OVER.**

bumped into Fran while shopping for clothes at Tower City. She had long freed herself of my dad and the addiction he lead her into. She looked healthy and happy. I was glad to see her in a better place in her life. Not all women make it out. I'd be finding that out very soon.

TAKING THE HOOD TO THE SUBURBS

White children were a thing heard of, but seldom seen, except on T.V. For us it was more like, 'In a galaxy far, far away, little Susie and little Johnny…" Our schools had the white teachers either unfortunate enough to delegated a position there or hopeful they could make a difference in the lives of a few inner city students. It was usually the former. Outside of interracial children, I didn't share a classroom with a white peer until 9th grade when I changed schools. If one or two of them were in my prior schools, they slipped my notice. Having so many of them around me was awkward. I stared at them; studied them the same way they studied me. I felt like an exhibit to them; something strange and distant, yet somehow similar.

This first major environmental and social change occurred in 2001 when I was 12-years-old. Crime and violence in our community turned it into more of a war zone than a residential area. Our home consisted of the elderly and a child. Elberon and E. 125th was no longer a place we could call home. My aunt sold the house and relocated us to Quilliams St. in what was then known as Cleveland Heights, a suburb. However, due to the technicality of my mother still having legal custody of me, I began attending Shaker Heights High. Shaker Heights High belonged to the district my mother resided in, courtesy of her section 8 voucher.

Shaker Heights High was an new experience for me. I was back in honors classes, but my new school's black population was 2%, at best. I didn't even bother trying to make friends. The ethnicities behaved in line with their stereotypes for the most part. I observed people, made a few random memories, and kept it moving. I wouldn't remember any of my classmates if I saw them today. My grandma gained custody pretty quickly, transferring me to Cleveland Heights High. I had been at Shaker Heights for a single month.

Regardless of where they moved me, I was determined to stay in contact with my old neighborhood. My route to the old stomping grounds included a long walk down Noble Rd. to reach east Cleveland. Then I'd have to catch the number six bus at Euclid, currently, the number 28, which they've split into two lines. I was reluctant to embrace the changes my new neighborhood introduced. Understanding the need for me to not only be removed from it, but the school system as well, my grandma and mother worked together to establish my grandma as my legal guardian. I was zoned for the new school system and life took on a different hue.

The thing about the suburbs in Cleveland, they don't last long. They are like a brand new, all white shirt made of poor material. As soon as it comes in contact with people, its decline is rapid. Section 8 was often the culprit. Bringing residents from disadvantaged backgrounds was deemed unfavorable for maintaining status. I won't lie. Part of Cleveland Heights's demise is credited to me and my generation. I took things over. It went from a quiet community to being off the hook. This occurred as soon as I met my new best friend, Katherine.

Like Tamira and I, conflict birthed our friendship. We were supposed to fight because no one had the opportunity to school her to who I was. No one there knew me so she couldn't ask about me. She had to learn the hard way and be the example for the neighborhood. See, Katherine had a little sister Jessica. Jessica had seen me hooping at the decrepit hoop attached to the house we moved into and the thought of bullying me dropped into her little ditzy head.

"Let me see your ball." The girl demanded. Mind you, she's younger than me.

So I'm like, "Fuck? No."

I believe, not sure, they had been familiar with the biracial children who occupied the home prior to us, Emma and Samantha. Katherine and her sisters were raised by their white family members. Perhaps Jessica assumed whatever softness ran rampant in that household rubbed off on whoever lived there, like some curse, but baby girl had it wrong. She and her sister were mixed as well, which contributed to their attitudes. They were mixed with boppers, or whores, and suburban bully, but if we are speaking race, they were black and white.

She proceeded to run her mouth and I proceeded to hoop as if she wasn't there, because for me she wasn't. We were raised with the belief white people were soft. They were not all white, but if you were mixed in the suburbs you were white. If you were mixed in the hood you were black. That was how it went. Considering them soft wasn't meant as a slight toward them. It was simply ignorance on our part. Just like their prejudice that we are dirty and incompetent.

After a bit, she decided to warn me when her big sister Katherine got released from jail I would be receiving my beat down. Long story short, Katherine got out. And she did make the walk down the street to confront me. But that's all she did. See, it was clear I wasn't from the suburbs. They were. Ain't shit shake. She was accustomed to people falling apart at the sight of her coming their way. They called her the Bully of the Burbs or Bopper. When she saw me she realized I was waiting for her to make the wrong move to street sweep the entire block with her. Instead, the conversation which ensued had no heat to it. However, I did like how she was able to pop off on everyone else so we got close. Not to mention, she became a source of cigarettes for me.

I had been smoking ever since my grandma started sending me to the corner store for her Winston 100's when I was 6-years-old. I would steal a few when I noticed her pack unattended. Also, my granddad smoked Salem 100's, my dad smoked Camels, my mom smoked Malboro 100's, Genie smoked Cools,

Jamiel smoked Newport 100's, and Terry smoked crack. So smoking found its way to me, or I found my way to each of their packs from time to time. I dug into everyone's stash except Terry's. That would never be for me.

Katherine, being two years older than I, was allowed to purchase cigarettes from the corner stores because she was well-known, making her an asset to me. Did you catch that? She was older than me by two years and had just gotten out of jail. Just some real insight into this chick. Moving along. She smoked Newport 100s which was fine with me. Being affiliated with her allowed me to get what I needed by association. We were inseparable, 365 days a year, no days off, no holidays.

I took my grandma's personal information without her knowledge or permission and went to the mall to buy two basic phones, one for me and one for Katherine. Yeah, I was bugging. Whatever I had, she had. If she was fighting, I was fighting. If she didn't like you, I didn't like you. If I didn't like you, she didn't like you. This was us. We even went on our dates together, whether the other person had a date or not. Third wheel didn't matter.

Katherine never gained the acceptance of my grandma. Being half white ruined any chance of her liking you. My grandma had an understandable aversion to whites, being born in 1928 Atlanta. I expect what she went through traumatized her to the point she didn't believe relations would ever change across races, no matter how superficially they masked things.

One day I had the nerve to make the mistake of a lifetime. Curiosity got the best of me and I invited a white boy over to teach me how to skateboard. I saw him doing it at school and intrigue took over. The habit of other communities caught my interest, mostly because it wasn't something I had exposure to. He came over and started showing me simple moves on the porch. Now remember, my grandma is the neighborhood watch all by herself. She was hanging out of the living room window and spotted us. Next thing we hear is her barreling onto the porch, demanding I get that 'honky' off her property. Yup. That was all she wrote.

To keep the peace, I only invited 'us' over to the house from that point forward, which meant I didn't have much company. Life changed so much for me after moving to the suburbs and meeting Katherine. For instance, when we first met I was still a virgin. I was fresh, but intact. There was this day we were coming from Joseph's place, one of her many sources of penis, down in East Cleveland. She was from the burbs but she only dealt with hood niggas. Typical. We were on our way home and this guy named JR offered us a ride. Hitchhiking was a dangerous gamble, but we took it. He was the only one I was interested in because he was one of the few she hadn't fucked, yet. Every time I would ask about a guy her response would be, "Fucked him". That was just her M.O. And if she hadn't, her sisters had. Boppers to the core.

Since JR hadn't been soiled he became my first at 13-years-old. He took an interest in me immediately after meeting me. I must have been an easy mark. JR had brown skin and a tongue ring, which was new to me. What was also new for me was his ability to pick me up and take me places. I felt like it was a big deal. It was my first time having a boyfriend able to do it. I also wasn't used to someone being as available for me. He would take me out to eat and sit on the phone talking to me. These simple things added up to him being the one I decided to lose my virginity to.

Here's how it went. Ketra still lived on the same block from our childhood and I asked him to take me by her house to see her one day. Things had been heating up between us for some time. I noticed him getting erect when I pressed my body up against his in a joking manner. He would reach under my shirt and squeeze my breast, sucking on my neck. It felt so good to me. His sucks sent electric tingles down my sides into my belly. It was only a matter of time. On the way to Ketra's I started rubbing on his crotch. He kept telling me not to start what I couldn't finish. I wasn't one to back down. I popped off at the mouth about being up for anything. He pulled his car right into the parking lot of a Christ The King Church. He parked his car in the back, against the building, in the cut facing forward to see if anyone approached. I slid into the back seat, pulled my pants and panties off, then got on my back.

"You got a condom?" I asked. We didn't plan this.

"Yeah." He said. "You want me to use it?"

"Hell yeah you gotta use it." I watched him slide the packet out of his jeans. It didn't dawn on me at the moment, but this nigga actually had a condom on standby, ready for action. Once wrapped, he lowered his body over mine and lifted one of my legs to gain access. He checked through the front windshield to make sure no one was approaching. After a couple of uncomfortable minutes, my virginity was gone.

It was kind of poetic. I lost my innocence in a place for innocence. I attended pre-school here. I gave up my goodies for the first time in a car like countless other girls. It being my first time, I had no idea what was going on. In fact, I thought we were having anal sex because the pain was in my butt, but we hadn't. That's just where I felt most of the pressure. I don't recall making it to Ketra's house that day.

JR was displeased about wearing a condom. I never met a guy who loved them. The ones who wore them without being asked didn't particularly enjoy them, they just understood what was lurking in these streets and in these sheets. The ones who made you stand your ground about wearing one, well, I considered them to be reckless as hell. The second they made a single objection I knew for sure they were the ones to be most concerned about. That meant they were slipping and sliding in everything unprotected that let them. Shit! Wouldn't take me out like that. That mess was just nasty.

I was very astute and understood the dangers of unprotected sex. I signed myself up with Planned Parenthood immediately after the experience as a preventative measure. It was wild because when they called the house they would give the name 'Nicki' as if they were your homegirl so your parents wouldn't be suspicious. I was getting all of my STD tests done and contraceptives without their knowledge. I planned to have sex often.

I'm glad I was aware enough to take care of myself, because after the casual encounter he vanished. Like, straight up disappeared. It was cool. I was young and it was what it was, but had I not protected myself, I could have been left traumatized by the situation.

Katherine, being the whore she was, made sure I didn't dwell on it too much. She was used to guys running through her. She told me niggas weren't shit. They came a dime a dozen. A new dude would be trying to holla at me in no time. I already knew all this. Hoe and all, she was my girl. JR had been the guy I was seeing, but your friends are the ones you are bound to.

Katherine and I grew so tight, when I got my first car, she would drive it while I was in school. Being her super dope self, she would have it cleaned for me whenever she had it. She even copped me a Tweety Bird steering wheel cover, floor mats, and accessories knowing how much I loved Tweety. She was my girl for real.

Why did Katherine have my car when I was in school when she should have been in school herself? Great question. Katherine didn't go to school. She was in and out of alternative institutions, mostly out. She reminded me of my father in that aspect. Street smart, high street cred, but not at all interested in being force fed state structured curriculums.

Every transition I made in life she was right there with me. I started dabbling in marijuana for income, not use. It wasn't immediately my thing. It made me paranoid. Over time I got used to it and it became a habit. Being a hustler and seeing how drugs moved, they became my next hustle. Katherine never had to pay for hers. I would smoke and hustle, hustle and smoke, with Katherine by my side the entire time.

I tried not to let all of my activity be illegal. The city of Cleveland Heights created a Chore Service program. Chore was a way for youth to earn income cleaning for the elderly. You applied at city hall and could earn five dollars and fifteen cents per hour, not to exceed three hundred dollars per month.

This was my first documented employment. It was simple enough. I received a list of elderly people. We came to an agreement on the dates, times, and hours they needed me and I cleaned their homes during those appointments. The majority of the family's who made the list were white.

The following year, when I was 14-years-old, I became employed with Brown & Wallace. This entailed me working on marketing projects with a woman in her basement. Unfortunately, she wanted me to sacrifice all of my dreams for her's and refused to become flexible in considering my basketball schedule. There was not much either of us could expect from the other in that situation. She had a business to run and I had a sport to train for.

My frequent visits to the old streets were against the wishes of my family. Still, my friends were there. My roots were there. I didn't know or fit in with these suburban kids, except Katherine. I missed Chris's car shop where I had gotten my rotts and the attached cleaners with its red brick that stood out to me when I was little. I missed the corner store my grandma sent me to for her beer and cigarettes. I missed Finast and how people had to help me find and reach items on my grandma's list when I was little. I remember wanting to try Aunt Jemima's syrup because a black lady's face was on it so I just knew it would be good, but I also knew if I brought any other syrup home beside Mrs. Butterworth, I would be sent right back to exchange it. It was the same with white bread. I only got to eat it when I went over my cousin's house or a friend's mother fed us while we played. On my grandma's counter was an old-fashioned, wooden bread box which was only allowed to store Home Pride wheat bread. You'd get words for anything else.

Then there was Renee's cleaners on 125th and Superior, where I worked from time to time when I needed cash. I missed my Elberon days. The quietness of the suburbs reverberated off of me. People owned more there so they stayed inside to enjoy their lives in peace. They didn't have to escape into the streets and mingle for entertainment.

The only resemblance of our old life in the suburbs was my dogs. Shaba impregnated another one of our dogs, Sparkle, a mini pincher my high school sweetheart Martel Mann gifted me for Christmas. The litter consisted of three puppies, Cochief, Blackey who was all black, and a third who died at birth. They turned the house all the way up. Cochief and Blackey wound up being bigger than Sparkle, but smaller than Shaba, and wilder than both. It was insane all the time with them, yet the thought of getting rid of them never crossed our minds. As wild as they were we loved them. There was never a dull moment.

Shaba proved to be the house whore because he also got Madalion pregnant, but we decided not to keep any of their puppies. Madalion expressed extreme resentment toward Sparkle and attacked her the moment she wasn't being supervised. It was sad. Madalion always had issues though. Roderick, a guy in his 20's I dated, gave her to me. He lived in the projects and bred pit bulls. She was useless to him because one of the three legs she did have had a birth defect. His only reason for breeding pits was profit. Knowing I cared for animals the way I did, he let me have her.

Our old neighborhood and people close to me were shaken again in 2002. I had actually been in the area when it happened. Ketra's old boo Brandon had been home when the tragic event took place. As I strolled closer to his house, I wasn't headed to see him but it was on the way to my destination, I noticed police cars and the coroner. A sickening feeling buried itself in the pit of my stomach. I knew the people who lived here; Brandon, his brother Luther, his sister Tasha, their mother Rose, and their step-dad. The step-dad was the type to let Rose know no good would come out of any attempts to leave him. The whole block knew this.

Tasha had been at her father's house and Luther was on Superior Hill with his cousin AJ on this particular day. Only Brandon, Rose, and his step-dad were at the house. Now Rose was a milk chocolate brick house. She stood 5'2 with all the right places on her body highlighted by curves and a nose ring like the cherry on top of her beauty. She was well-known and beloved in our part of town. You either knew her because she worked at the cable company and would hook you up with a pay-per-view connection to watch the fights or because she did everyone's hair. The children loved her also. She kept her nails done and would paint the nails of any little girl in the neighborhood whose parents allowed it. Their living room had an arcade Pac-Man game all the community youth would stop by and play from time to time. You didn't even have to put money in it. You just played.

Well, Rose's desire to be free of her boyfriend must have been stronger than her fear of any of his threats because she told him she was leaving. She went to a local bar for a few drinks, then went to see Nellie's mom. Nellie was Brandon's current girlfriend. He tracked Rose to Nellie's house, banged on the door, kicked it in and dragged her out of it and down the street. This scene took me back to when my dad did basically the same thing to Fran. You would think with so many people outside watching this someone would have intervened. But no. All the dope boys hyped each other up and agreed this was how you had to treat these 'bitches' nowadays.

So Rose gets pulled into the house and taken into the bedroom where a fight ensues. At some point, someone noticed he had a gun and called 9-1-1. The protect and serves didn't respond for over two hours. Long story short, he shot Rose in the head as she scrambled for the door, then he buried a bullet in his own skull. Brandon escaped by jumping off of the roof of the house trying to get help. He ran up the hill to get Luther, but it was too late. It was all just a mess.

I couldn't believe it was unreal. Sadness consumed me as they brought Rose out in a body bag and pronounced her dead. When the article came out in the paper, I cut it out and kept it. I still have it. They ruled it a homicide-suicide. There were an alarming amount of incorrect statements regarding Rose's murder. I don't know if it was due to conflicting witness statements or

THEY RULED IT A HOMICIDE-SUICIDE.

indifference to events in the hood. It felt like what Doughboy said in Boyz-N-The Hood, "Either they don't know, don't show, or don't care about what's going on in the hood." One detail which emerged during the investigation deepened the sadness of our tight-knit community. The boyfriend kept a journal. His plan was to kill the children as well. They escaped that fate by not being home and Brandon by reaching the roof.

Tasha's father took custody of her, but Brandon and Luther went to two separate homes. Understandably, nothing was ever the same for him. I ran into Brandon seven years later on the bus. I made sure not to mention anything surrounding his mother or the events of that day, even though it was my first time seeing him since. That had to be the worst day of his life and I wasn't going to be the one to make him relive it. I wondered often if the police had responded timely, like they do for white neighborhoods, if Brandon would still have his mother.

Life continued teaching me about the ditches I would find myself in if I didn't stay on the right path. Will lived ten blocks from my home on Quilliams. I started seeing him when I was 14-years-old. Will was 19. We were getting it in on the regular early in our 'relationship'. Once I got a taste of sex it was a wrap. I liked everything about it, especially if the guy half knew what he was doing.

Looking back, I can admit being a bit out of control. I didn't sleep at home every night like a 14-year-old should. I packed a bag and spent a night, or week, in different places. Will's place was one. Whenever I decided to go home he walked with me. I'll never forget one walk in particular. I felt weird the entire way home. I hadn't been to the house in a few days. I figured it would be best if I snuck in my window to avoid being seen. I had to go to the bathroom so bad I barely said bye to Will.

As soon as I sat on the toilet, my painful urination almost catapulted me straight off. It took me a minute to add two and two together. I visited 'Nicki' the next day. Since I enrolled myself when I lost my virginity, I knew they would test me without my guardian's knowledge or consent. There was no way I was telling my family I thought I had an STD. I got tested and waited for the call to tell me what I already suspected. A few days later, confirmation rang. Will gifted me a twofer, chlamydia and trichomoniasis. How generous of him.

I picked up the antibiotics and dealt with it in silence. Will had been around my family for the holidays and they didn't mind us dating, even with the age difference. I just didn't want to deal with hearing how careless I had been. Needless to say, we ended up splitting. Yet, Will obviously hadn't had enough of my family. It would take two years of my mother smiling in my face and gloating about her new boyfriend Will before a sick truth came to light.

The older I got and the more shit I got into, the more I started realizing I needed to chill the fuck out. My circle started getting smaller and my priorities began changing. Things that excited me before no longer had the same appeal. My bond with Keisha in those days caused us to behave more like sisters. I had to be 15-years-old when we got into an altercation walking to Save-A-Lot, similar to Aldi's. There was a group of kids matching our stride on the opposite side of the street. I knew one of the girls so we paid them no attention. She didn't scare me, but she wasn't alone. The fact she was in a group made me cautious. People moving in a group acted differently than they would if they rolled solo. They operated under a pack mentality.

We kept walking without paying them any obvious attention. Then the words floated across the street, letting me know they were dead set on causing trouble. I just wanted to get to Save-A-Lot for my generic Kool-Aid packs.

"Aye!" A voice shouted louder than necessary to ensure we heard it. "Look at that bitch."

I never missed a step, never turned my head. Bitch this and bitch that was part of our daily vernacular. I'd been called one before, did my share of calling bitches bitch, and knew this was an attempt to bait me in. I had no issue with fighting, but we were outnumbered, and I simply wasn't in the mood for anything else but cherry Kool-Aid.

"You just gonna let them talk to you like that?" Keisha knew me and was shocked I wasn't halfway across the street to knock off the head of whoever made the statement.

Keisha's statement irritated me. Not only were there more of them than us, she couldn't fight. What bothered me, even more, was she wasn't so ready to fight when people stepped solely to her. I always jumped in and fought with her if I was around so she didn't get molly whopped. So if I did engage, I had no real backup. She wouldn't sit on the sidelines of course, but she wouldn't be much help. Keisha pushed a button though. I couldn't let my cousin see me get punked.

I said fuck it and spazzed on everyone. The girl who knew me refused to fight because she had respect for me. The others didn't know any better. They cursed her out and called her all types of punk bitches and raggedy so and so, but she remained on the side, preferring their antagonistic remarks to my fists. I gave Waliah, the ring leader, an Ieshia special which always shatters the confidence of the pack. Too busy running her mouth, she couldn't get out of the way fast enough to escape my right hook. Waliah stumbled back. My second blow hit her right on the top of her head, forcing her to the ground. It looked like I was playing Whack A Mole. With there being so many of them, I had to get them

> IT WOULD TAKE TWO YEARS OF MY MOTHER SMILING IN MY FACE AND GLOATING ABOUT HER NEW BOYFRIEND WILL BEFORE A SICK TRUTH CAME TO LIGHT.

out of the way quickly before they all ganged up on me. I felt a few tugs on me from different directions and threw a few wild punches to fend them off. A couple of hits landed, but none were enough to take me down. I fought my way out of the cloud of assailants, creating distance between myself and them. I looked around to see Keisha's status. She was trying to untangle herself from the clutches of two girls, banging against her with furious blows. I went over and kicked one of them off her, startling the other. The group backed away, talking mad shit like they got the win. I didn't care. It was over. I wasn't hurt, Keisha was ok, and I could continue on to my Kool-Aid.

Hearing my cousin question whether I would respond to the verbal attack or not made me think of how the streets would feel if they heard I let it slide. It was more than just my cousin's opinion. My entire street cred was placed in jeopardy. The sensation of not wanting to fight was weird for me because I was a fighter. But I honestly wanted to avoid the whole instance for once. To my chagrin, the run in with Waliah started a chain of events. She lived two blocks up from Quilliams on Noble Rd. From the fight on, every time I saw her at the bus stop I wanted wreck, meaning to beat that ass. And anytime one of my people saw her out and about, they called me to notify me of her location and I came running.

Age fifteen wound up being a more pivotal stage in my life than expected. I wasn't grown, but you couldn't tell me that. I started asking my family about a vehicle so I could get around more conveniently. I knew I was a year too young to get one. The idea still needed to be discussed so they could start working on it. I knew the streets and the transit system like the back of my hand. It was how the youth of the inner city grew up. A car afforded me the option of more than my immediate surroundings. Our parents couldn't afford to gift us BMWs or Volvos or Benzs on our sweet sixteens. If we wanted to somewhere we hopped on public transportation. We had been doing it all of our lives from early ages. Hell, most of our parents still rode it. So it was whatever that I had to continue riding one until my time to get a car came around.

Unfortunately, a catch 22 of the independence urban youth experience and the higher level of public interaction is the exposure to danger. There I was standing on the corner of Quilliams St. waiting for the bus when my life changed. See, you have to realize at any moment while you breathe, things can happen to alter the course and quality of your life forever. You may not see the window of opportunity, doesn't mean it doesn't see you. You will be amazed at how quickly minor encounters spiral out of control. The point is, people and entities are always lurking, preying, laying in wait to snatch the unsuspecting.

The F-150 crew cab rolled up to me. It had a flatbed with two seats in the front and two in the rear. A man who could have been my uncle, or the uncle of any other girl I knew, started with the typical line of interrogation.

"Where you going?" He called out of his window, arm rested in the open frame.

"To get my hair done." I responded. At the time, my hair was fuschia. High school was a period of experimenting with a variety of colors.

"Let me give you a ride." He smiled. "You too cute to be catching the bus."

Now, I'm a hustler, and I'm from the streets so this didn't impress me at all. Catching the bus was fine. I sized him up, calculating if further discussion was even worth my time.

"You wanna buy some weed?" I shot back. Might as well make some change if I was going to let him spend a few minutes with me. He told me to get in and he would see what I had. I hopped into the truck. Kelley played nice for the few miles and delivered me as promised to the salon. I gave him a five dollar half gram bag to try. In the hood we called them five dolla hollas. He suggested we exchange numbers which led to him picking me up at school from time to time. Young and naïve, I felt super dope having this grown ass man coming for me with my peers seeing us together.

I guess Kelley decided he had warmed me up to him enough because he called one night with this bright idea for me to make money.

"Why can't you just tell me?" I asked irritated.

"This ain't something you talk about on the phone baby girl." He wanted to discuss it in person. I agreed. He picked me up an hour later. Remember, my grandma was up there in age and not really mobile so it was easy for me to come and go. Still, I met him around the corner. I wasn't brazen enough to have him pull up to the front door.

I ask Kelley what the money making idea is and he starts with how he has these guys. Then I'm just hearing words in clusters like, "you're their type", and "it'll be at my house", "I'll be there the whole time", "discreet", 'casual', and "more money than selling weed".

I was caught all the way off guard. No one could have prepared me for the proposition. Now, hooking was something I caught glimpses of, never something I thought I would engage in. I told Kelley I didn't know if I wanted to partake in the offer. When I met him I told him I was 18-years-old because that's how the game is played. I'm sure he knew I wasn't, but I'm also sure he didn't know how young I actually was. To be honest, I don't think he cared. Here was this young girl in the streets unaccompanied, able to leave her home at all hours of the night. I was a prime candidate. He downplayed the hell out of the situation and told me it would only be a 'little' sex here and there.

"It's not hooking." He explained. I wouldn't be on the corner late at night in neon fishnet tights, high heels and caked on makeup.

After losing my virginity I became promiscuous and sex itself didn't bother me. Kelley must have seen the wheels spinning. He started sounding like an interviewer going over qualifications. "You have to be able to suck dick and swallow."

"Hell no!" I exploded. "That's terrible." I couldn't imagine.

"Hold up." He said, attempting to make me calm down.

"Have you ever tried?" He asked.

"No and I don't want to." I said.

"How do you know you won't like it? We gonna try it." See, the thing about a predator is they are skilled in dealing with their prey and taking control of the situation when it may spring from the trap.

Kelley told me we were going to pull into a secluded area off the road. I was to suck his dick and see if I survived the swallowing part. I did, barely, after holding and turning it over in my hands for inspection. I needed to ensure there were no sores on that thing. I saw those pictures in Sex Ed. No thanks. He cocked his head to the side and looked at me like I had the nerve. Yes the hell I did have the nerve to inspect a dick headed for my mouth! I acted just like I didn't notice him and finished my inspection before bending over into his anxious lap. His balls had a slight twinge of musk to them, which nearly canceled the entire training session. Kelley's dick wasn't so big that I couldn't hold it in my mouth. I gagged a few times, but that was more from him getting excited and shoving it further down my throat than I was ready for without warning. He kept telling me if I relaxed it would slide to the back of my throat easier. He went on to say I was the best and all other hype. When he came, the consistency almost took me out. It was like swallowing thick, creamy, unsweetened oatmeal-slimy.

"I definitely have some people for you. I knew you would be good when I first saw those dsl's." He nodded more to himself than me as he removed tissue from the glove compartment, wiped off the residual, and zipped his pants up. I wondered if the fact that he had tissue in his glove compartment was a testament to the frequency of these instances or if tissue was just something he kept handy.

"What are dsl's?" I asked.

"Dick sucking lips." He smiled. Here we go. I had heard people make the reference without knowing what it meant.

My first 'client' was an African guy he orchestrated a sexual encounter for at an unfurnished house. Yeah, I took him up on the offer. At fifteen I was wise enough to know how to take care of myself in the streets and make the best decisions for me, right? I knew enough about life to know what I was doing, right? Looking back on the structures he took me to for the transactions, I think he invested in fixer uppers and flipped them. The place obviously was not his residence, but he had access to it. The only furnishing was a twin bed in one of the bedrooms. Kelley led us to it and left us to transact. The service paid sixty dollars, half staying with me, half going to Kelley. At that moment I realized his role as the manager, or pimp. He asked how it made me feel and I told him it was 'whatever'. I had a habit of using the term when I was nervous or uncomfortable. He knew what it was. He wasn't new to this. I wondered how many other girls and women he had done this to and how long he had been at it. When he handed my money to me he told me I could make even more than that. For my vagina? I would hope so.

The next encounter was with another African man and his friend. They wanted a threesome. Kelley advised this was one of the ways he was referring to when he mentioned I could make more money. The thoughts running through my mind this time were different from the first incident. The first time I was caught up in the experience. Having sex for funds instead of leisure was new for me. But prostitution was an industry well before flipping burgers.

Wives. Girlfriends. Social status. Twirling in my mind while they were pounding their heavy pelvises against mine were images of their significant others, out and about, either clueless or fully aware of their perverse habit. Were they still getting down in the sheets at home? Were they happy? Did they both sleep with other people? Was the money they spent on my goodies taking food off the table, gas out of the tank, or delaying the payment of a bill?

I felt dirty and culpable for unknown wrongs when it was over. Even worse, the last client started stalking me. He approached me at my house one day and asked if we could spend time together. His thing had been cruising through my neighborhood on weekends, hoping to catch me outside. I told him where I lived during some small talk we had prior to sex. It didn't cross my mind he planned to use the information.

"Are you a citizen?" I asked.

"What do you mean?" He laughed at the question.

"I know sometimes y'all need to marry someone to get citizenship and stay." I stared out of the passenger side window, watching cars and buses flow through the arteries of the city.

"I'm American baby girl." He turned to stare at me in an attempt to convey sincerity. "I don't need marriage to stay." His accent still very thick. Thanks to his years speaking English I could understand him, but it sounded as if he might break into a rash of Yoruba at any moment.

"Good because I'm not trying to marry anyone." I said.

"You're too young for marriage." He laughed again.

"I don't know how it works. You could propose an arrangement for when I turn 18." I wasn't dumb. I knew they finagled things when need be. "I heard y'all pay people to do it."

"No baby. You have me wrong." His demeanor turned serious. He didn't want me to think poorly of him. "When I marry I want to marry for love. I'm free to marry who I want and you are free to marry who you want. I just like spending time with you right now. What's all the marriage talk? You want to marry me?" He was teasing, trying to get me off of the topic.

"Depends." I looked him dead in his eyes. "How much would I get paid to marry someone who needed citizenship? Would I get more than I make for my pussy?"

He laughed again, uneasily shifting in his seat. "I don't know these things. I've never done it before, so I don't know.

I sat there chewing on the information, considering if I had other questions. I decided not. What was the point? I wasn't going to marry someone so they could get citizenship. That would interfere with my real life too much. What if I fell in love with someone else? How would I explain that? What would he think of me? Then there was the fact he was a citizen so he didn't need me anyway.

I agreed to see him on the side in my free time. Shit. I already fucked him. Funny thing is we didn't do anything else. He seemed to just like my appearance and want company. Perhaps it was a rule for him not to go behind Kelley's back for a transaction. I didn't know at the time, but my instincts were right.

Naivety caused me to feel empowered, being paid for my body. I was engaged in lewd acts for profit and no one knew it besides Kelley, myself, and my clients. Why work like a dog for five dollars and fifteen cents an hour when I can make in ten minutes what that would earn in a day, plus some.

I wound up telling Kelley about seeing the guy on the side. He was bent out of shape at the fact I was alone with him. He made it about being concerned for my well-being and me not being taken advantage of, but game recognized game. He didn't want to be cut out of a transaction. It was my vagina after all. I didn't need a middle man to manage or profit off of it. Anyway, I only saw the guy on the side maybe three times at the most before I cut him off.

The trips with Kelley for our 'clients' continued. The next man he took me to service was older than I had ever had before, but he wasn't elderly. He was just older. This dude tried me. He decided he didn't want to use a condom.

"Aww man! Come on!" His theatrical pleading irritated me a bit. "Kelley said it would be alright."

"I don't care what Kelley said." I looked him dead in his face with my eyebrows raised to drive the point home. "It's definitely not alright and we're definitely not rolling like that."

He wanted pussy so he got with the program. When it was all said and done, he gave me a half ounce of weed. Now, I'm sitting here thinking in my mind, *What the fuck is going on? Is he really trying to pay me for sex in marijuana?*

He goes back into his song and dance about Kelley saying it was okay. I knew right then and there something was up and this wasn't going to work for me. The damn weed wasn't even high grade. He tried to pay me for my body with some garbage. I let that be the last time Kelley and his friends had access to me. In the back of my mind I couldn't help but think this was his way of getting back at me for spending time with the African without his permission.

To this day, I still cross distant paths with Kelley. He'll be out and about with his family and I'll wonder if they know about his shady dealings. This man, smiling in his wife's face and being a father to his children, out here pimping young girls and training them in his truck? And though I haven't spoken with him in years, the sight of him makes me ill. Immediately upon seeing him, fear and shame overtake me. His image, even his memory, bring everything back as vivid as if I just lived it. I would take it all back if I could, but that's life.

I'm not sure why in the world I was so reckless. Let's blame it on youth and ignorance. What I failed to consider through my entire sex service career was the risk of being found out by other means. Any friends of my parents could have spotted me riding around with him and snitched. Or better yet, anyone could have been on the other side of the door when I showed up to an appointment. I didn't know everyone my parents knew. Lucky for me, I never bumped into anyone who recognized me.

Coming out on the other end of that traumatic experience I realized I needed to double down and keep my shit together and moving forward. I got a job working at Subway in Richmond Mall and served at Carl's on Noble Rd. on Sundays and evenings, if I had free time. I didn't mind working because I liked making my own money. I especially didn't mind working at Carl's because it was a black owned restaurant and I learned a lot of skills while working there. I loved making cash tips and my famous banana pudding recipe came from my days there.

After that I took a position making five dollars and fifteen cents an hour at Burger King on Cedar Rd., saving all my pennies for my first car. The car I

> **THIS MAN, SMILING IN HIS WIFE'S FACE AND BEING A FATHER TO HIS CHILDREN, OUT HERE PIMPING YOUNG GIRLS AND TRAINING THEM IN HIS TRUCK?**

asked my family for months ago. Burger King replaced Subway because the Arabian owner was wicked. He failed to take into consideration my age and made demands on me that often lead to me reminding him. His response to my refusal to work shifts which compromised my academics or sports was to cut my hours altogether.

Bud, my play-play big brother, lived in Little Mexico, the apartments across the street from the Burger King where I worked. Its dense Mexican population earned it the name. You heard more Spanglish than English if you stood outside. His mother was on Section 8 so he didn't have to kick in much to stay there. Oddly, and common enough for teens nearly the age of maturity, his mother didn't occupy the premises. She had her own place. Bud was 17-years-old, but his classes were remedial so his school schedule was different from mine. His mom didn't want him living under her roof with his behavior challenges. It was her way of promoting his independence and self-development.

When I first got this job I had no idea how much the location would work out for me. Bud and his friends came through and got free food if I was on the clock. Anyone who works in fast food can relate. You give free food to your people when you see them if you can. You know how the system works.

On the flip side, I stayed at Bud's house when suspended from school. At this point I considered myself completely independent. Shit, I was fucking and had sold my pussy for money. I wasn't taking shit from anyone which resulted in school fights getting me expelled. I saw no reason to sit home during suspension. My go-to was working additional shifts in that free time. If no shifts were available, Bud let me hang out with him and his friends so I didn't have to wander the streets or get lectured at home.

We both attended Cleveland Heights High. That's how we met. He was part of the G-Square Boyz, which didn't bother me because Cleveland is overrun by gangs. Everyone you knew was either in a gang or connected to one in some way. He became affiliated with them because his best friend Mal G ran it. Mal G was currently doing an extensive bid in prison. I never affiliated myself with any real ones, but I was comfortable having friends who did. Martell, Bud's real name, wasn't a banger in my eyes. This is not my high school sweetheart, Martel, but they shared similar features and the same name spelled differently. He too had green eyes, but light skin. Sandy brown waves crowned his head.

Not many understood how to maintain a relationship with him. He exhibited bipolarity which kept him in his own zone, but for the most part, he was cool as shit. I was a people person, so it wasn't difficult for me to figure out how to get along with anyone. I also respected his space. He kept headphones on to listen to music and recorded all the drama he found, especially street brawls after school. A thing in the hood was to find a white boy and steal on him, meaning knock him out with a punch to the face. Whenever he caught wind one was about to go down, he made sure to get on the scene and record it to watch later. Someone found out he was doing this and an investigation started that led to the confiscation and destruction of the footage.

Of course our friendship involved us having sex from time to time, but we kept it on the low. No one at school would have guessed what was happening since it wasn't meant to be all that. His best friend Razul caught on, but it's hard to hide stuff like that from people who are always with you. He never said anything to anyone though because he knew we weren't planning to get serious. I'm sure Bud appreciated it. If people caught wind that we were messing around, it could have interfered with him entertaining other girls. Seeing as clingy or needy wasn't my thing, there was no need for all that. He was free to do what and who he wanted. We were friends with benefits and that worked for us.

I knew Cleveland and its people inside and out: the degenerates, the uppity, the hood and the well-off. I knew how to maneuver, how to run with the Bud's and Ketra's, the Kelley's and the Katherine's. I wanted more though. This couldn't be it for me. I needed to expand my territory and meet different people with different ways of thinking and living. I needed to grow.

My family previously promised to help me get a vehicle once I turned fifteen and knew I needed them to enroll me in driver's education, but neither happened. Not one to keep asking for help, I was forced to take matters into my own hands. Patience was never a virtue I possessed. When it was time to enroll in driver's education, I forged my grandma's signature without a second thought and paid the fee from what I had saved up. The instructor picked me up from my house and I commenced my 8 hours of on the road and 24 hours in the class training. Since I didn't have my car yet, I capitalized on the ability to drive Fox's car. He was my on and off boo thing. Fox would scoop me up and let me drive while we were in the streets doing whatever we were into for the day.

The money I was making was trickling in slower than I liked. My mind started going to unsavory places in an attempt to get enough money for anything reliable. Fox helped me come up with a sketchy hustle to get the money I needed to buy a car.

It took a few weeks for my scheme to land me the money for the car. Once I had it, Fox took me to 106th and Superior where he heard a guy was selling a '90 Cutlass Ciera. We registered it in Fox's name at first due to my age and I drove it on 30-day tags. As soon as I turned sixteen we transferred it to my name.

When I first saw the Ciera, I thought it looked like a blue metal rectangle. Thinking back on it makes me laugh because the front seat was a bench, meaning if one person moved either end of the seat forward, the entire front row shifted forward. Whenever I had people in it with me someone always had something to say if the seat moved and no one was ever in agreement with moving it in the first place.

Shortly after acquiring the vehicle the brakes went out on my drive to school. I almost lost my life. I couldn't drive it until the brakes were fixed. If it wasn't one thing it was another. The repairs were to the tune of two hundred forty dollars. I didn't have it. Basketball season had started so I wasn't working. I made it a point to prioritize keeping my grades high and attending practice which left little time or energy for work. Whatever I earned during the off-season I saved in reserve for when I wasn't working during the season. At most I had thirty dollars to my name up to this point. Then again, how hard would it be for a hustler like me to flip thirty dollars into two hundred forty? Luckily my school had a shop so I left the car there. I called my aunt Genie and got her to take me to Sam's Club to pick up boxes of candy. I sold them at school and got her to take me back for a few more boxes. I was still a little short of my goal. On the way, she decided to ask if I was going to get my grandma a pack of cigarettes. I assume my grandma had put in a request before she picked me up and this was her way of broaching the subject.

"I'm not getting her no cigarettes." I answered.

Genie went off. "All the shit she's done for y'all and you can't buy her any cigarettes?" She ranted, in her raspy voice very akin to my own, about how ungrateful the members of our family were.

This didn't move me. I could hear another of my grandma's favorite lines roaring in my head. *I don't have to do anything but be black and die!* I reiterated my position and told her smoking was my grandma's habit and it was up to her to support her habits. I had my own bills to take care of. I was a believer in being responsible for your own choices. For instance, I was currently wearing a pair of braces for which I was paying two hundred and twenty-nine dollars a month.

My refusal to acquiesce inspired her to reach over and punch me in the mouth, full of said braces. Immediately my lips began swelling. I was floored. Reflexes and principle got her served a face full of retributive pounding. This taught me something about my aunt. She meant well for the most part, but her giving wasn't selfless. It was calculated and she kept a running tab to hold over your head. Whenever she didn't agree with your choices, she expressed her opinion, welcomed or not. And she always had an opinion about everyone's life which kept her gossiping. Other people's business was constantly flowing out of her mouth. She didn't have much life experience to speak from because she was never in the streets so her views came from a haughty perspective without anything else behind it except unfounded judgment. Her demeanor came across as if she thought she was better than you. This was what most people disliked about her. She didn't care. She'll tell you to this day she doesn't care who doesn't like her and why.

Even as my mother endured her recovery from addiction, she lured her past over her and became a stumbling block. That day in the car with her taught me to just take her for what she is and ignore the noise. My dad would say this is where she got her joy from since she didn't have a family or life of her own. I don't totally agree with it, but I do know people who aren't happy in their personal lives try to make others unhappy. Misery loving company and all.

> MY REFUSAL TO ACQUIESCE INSPIRED HER TO REACH OVER AND PUNCH ME IN THE MOUTH, FULL OF SAID BRACES.

Personally, I was far from miserable. I was fortunate enough to be enraptured with my high school sweetheart, Martel Mann. Guys my age didn't appeal to me in the least bit. Martel was 18-years-old and I was super into him. His mom, however, was very opposed to our situation. As a mother now, I can understand her position. If anything had gone wrong he could've been charged with statutory rape. And when she found out we were indeed very sexually active, shit hit the fan. She spazzed all the way out. It didn't unhinge us though. We expected it because of her clear disapproval of us from the beginning. Eventually, when she realized we weren't breaking up, and we weren't going to stop having sex, she got over it.

In fact, we started spending time together. His mother was in her 40's, but she wore clothes girls my age wore. She also acted similar to girls my age. We picked out belly shirts and shorts together, the whole nine. I didn't pick up on how hood and immature she was because I was so blissfully wrapped up in her son. I thought, silly me, that we were bonding and things would be fine. Silly me.

She was a brown skinned, nice looking woman. She loved gold. She had gold teeth and wore lots of gold jewelry. Being born and raised in the United Kingdom, a thick British accent carried her words from lip to ear. A pointed Euro nose set off her unique traits. Men loved her. She kept a flock at her beck and call.

This was the weirdest thing his mom and I had in common. Tongue rings. She enjoyed displaying hers, especially around young dudes. She had a thing for the ones born and raised in the hood. I got mine as a result of my mom's attempts to get me on her good side. She took me to get my tongue pierced. I had been asking and she picked me up one day to take me on the bus out to Wickliffe.

Martel took after her. He inherited the nose and caramel tone. Like lots of children, he had been chubby, thinning throughout his high school years. He kept his gorgeous waves in a sandy brown, low cut fade. The features that struck you most were his green eyes and baby soft, pink lips. Man, those lips.

What sucks the most about breakups is when the issue doesn't originate between the two parties. An external force permeated our relationship. Martel called me one day. His mother put him up to asking me for some money. They were getting evicted. It was a Saturday.

Me, being young, dumb, and in love, agreed to loan his mother fifteen hundred dollars to prevent the pending disaster. I saved this money working at Six Flags to buy my school attire. I didn't have to work. My aunt Genie would have gotten the clothes for me, but I loved getting what I wanted and not what someone wanted to give me. The terms of the loan were that my money would be repaid Thursday. She set up these terms. Thursday comes. Thursday goes. No money. Another Thursday passes by. I inquire about my money. What transpires? This chick gets an attitude. Same chick I had been shopping and bonding with.

It wasn't just because it was my money she was playing with that pissed me off. It was what I had to go through to earn it. The fourteen hours a day under the blistering, summer sun. The early mornings I endured and the lengthy, tedious hour bus ride to Six Flags from Van Aken.

Martel belonged in this fake gang called the Noble Boyz, but he wasn't hard like that. He was a good guy. Instead of keeping him out of it, his mother put him in a position that made him have to choose sides. A super momma's boy, he chose her even though he knew she was dead wrong. They were a close family and ride-or-die as families should be.

The series of unfortunate events which followed would have led you to believe I was beefing with a girl my own age. She proceeded with trying to have me jumped at school for wanting my money back. This led to me fighting with Martel in school, splashing him in the face with orange juice, and dumping a trash bin over his head. I then stole Carlton's bike, his little brother, and hid it behind a local CVS. Looking back, I realize the pettiness behind the move, but it ruffled their feathers and pissed them all the way off. Here I was going at it with his mother and brother, now I drag Carlton in the mess. But to be fair, he deserved a taste too. He mouthed off in the background whenever I called the house. A few times he even walked by my house shouting defamatory remarks. His mother had him present each time she tried to get me jumped, and the only reason I didn't lay hands on him was that he was so much younger than me. He couldn't get away with it all though. I made it a teachable moment for him that if you inject yourself into a situation, you would suffer the same consequences as everyone else. Obviously his family wasn't teaching him right so I was happy to oblige. The bonus was how upset they were Carlton was targeted; the precious baby of the family.

Now, while the RTA was a public transit, it operated similar to a school bus because its route was only for the schools. His mother kicked her antics into high gear, gathering some fake hood chicks from Alabama on multiple occasions, paying their fare just so they could ride my RTA route to jump me. I was blown. She borrowed money from me. A child. Her son's girlfriend because she couldn't pay her bills, and this was how she carried it in the end.

Grown as she was, his mother even resorted to playing on my phone. I doubt she would have done it if she had to call the landline at the house, but she knew my bedroom had its own line. I got tired of my grandma picking up a line from another room when I got calls and listening in or embarrassing me by yelling, "Get the fuck off the phone!" whenever she wanted so I got my own line. Had she called Ruth's line she would have gained a foe she didn't bargain for.

"Don't call my motherfucking house!" Would be the warning for calling for anyone other than her regardless of the time of day. If his mother felt froggy and said some smart shit, Ruth would have invited her over to resolve the matter.

It bruised me so deeply she went to all these lows to hurt me. I really cared for Martel and he cared for me. When things calmed down we discussed trying to be together, and we did. We tried. But it was impossible with what his mother did. I couldn't see her and me getting over what happened. Proving me right, she continued trying to get me jumped every chance she got.

Our fate was sealed when I caught her at the BP gas station. I approached her and asked her what was up since she was always trying to get me jumped. She had the problem with me, not the girls she was siccing on me. She must have heard about me in the streets because it wasn't her desire to fight me one on one, but I was in her face and there was no escaping it. So, I beat that ass Ieshia style. Man, I gave it to her with passion. I was finally getting my hands on her after all that time and ruining things for me and her son. I had a lot of anger to take out on her. After that, there was no coming back for Martel and me. The momma's boy couldn't look me in the face after what I did to his mother.

The drama still wasn't over. While Martel and I were in limbo I messed with a guy named Donnie. To teach Martel's family a lesson, Donnie and his boys kicked in their front door and pillaged the entire house. Stripped them bare. You could never have told me things would go this far. It wasn't something I asked him to do, but guys tend to go the extra mile for females they claim. This was his way of being protective and making the statement that no one messed with me without repercussions. I got questioned by the police. Thankfully nothing came of the investigation.

Martel, his mother, Carlton, and I were not the only ones to suffer behind my unreturned funds. Katherine was dating Martel's best friend Duck. Being my best friend, her allegiance was unwavering to me. Their relationship dissolved due to the conflict.

For my own personal revenge against Martel, because what I did to his mother was for her, not him, I went into my arsenal. Girls love playing with their guys and taking pictures when they are together. When Martel would visit me, he let me put makeup on him and dress him up. My phone was full of snaps of him with makeup and fur hats. I printed and posted my catalog on every bus stop I passed near the school and on every locker. I showed up early to ensure I was there before the bell rung so everyone would see it before he did and ripped them down. This wasn't a good look for any man, especially where I'm from. On top of it, his green eyes caused a higher level of issues for him. His mother was pissed. I was satisfied.

Some time had passed without any major drama in my life or my family's. I woke one Saturday and bounced downstairs to raid the refrigerator. *Ring!* It was the house phone. I couldn't be bothered to pick it up. I was too hungry. Plus, it was her line. I had my own. The ringing stopped after a second and I assumed my grandma answered it. Pulling the door to the refrigerator open, then leaning forward to closely inspect the contents, I nearly knocked myself unconscious when I heard my grandma yell.

"What happened!?" There was panic in her voice. "Is she okay?"

Hunger was still banging around my stomach walls, but concern diluted it. I headed upstairs.

"What's wrong?" I asked. She waved a hush my way so I sat on the foot of her bed and waited.

"Where is she?" She asked the caller. "Good. Oooh, she's lucky." A few moments later.

When the call was over I got the information. Keisha, learning I had purchased a car, convinced our uncle Jamiel to get her one. For some unknown, reason he obliged. I guess for the same reason I got the Coach bag when I was 11-years-old. Now, Keisha had no license, and absolutely no on the road training. Still, since I had a car she couldn't go on without having one herself. I think the fact that she was older than me really did it for her. Mind you, I asked for them to get my car but had to hustle for it myself. No more than twelve hours after getting the vehicle she wrecked it. She miraculously escaped injury. That was the main thing. I never understood why Keisha felt she had to keep up with me. I had my reasons for needing a car and they were very different from hers. I considered Keisha to have low self-esteem and figured she was just trying to follow in my steps.

Somehow, Keisha and I slowly drifted apart and had gone our separate ways for a while in the following years. I didn't see our split coming. It was only recently that we reached out to each other and started making an effort to catch up and reestablish our relationship. It's been fascinating and we have both missed too much in each other's lives.

My mother came around frequently, but seldom alone. Ricky, her husband, always shadowed her when she was out and about. They got married when I was eleven. My sister Diamond was born shortly after. I resented my mother for having her for a while. Here I was, almost grown and she goes off to have a baby when she didn't even commit to raising me. Yeah, I was all the way irritated with her. How dare she decide to be a mother to my sister but not me? What was the difference? I had been the only child all this time. She could have simply invested more into me if she felt she had more time and energy all of a sudden. I wasn't the only one who felt this way. My grandma echoed my sentiments constantly. Aunt Genie just found it amusing. Her take on it was my mother expected my grandma to 'rescue' Diamond from her as she had done with me, but girlfriend played herself. My grandma was more aged than when she took me on and wasn't raising any more children at such a young age on her own. They literally begged her not to have my baby sister.

My outrage at my mother for deciding to keep Diamond turned into pity for Diamond. She had it the worst. She was in and out of foster care and never got the chance to secure a good education. And as if all of that wasn't enough, the poor thing was abandoned to family or friends of our mother's whenever Deedee needed to be free or couldn't manage her.

Ricky, her father, was the true definition of a hater. This guy of hers had the nerve to be jealous of her 15-year-old daughter. I have no idea why. It wasn't like I was taking any of her time or money away from him. Then the truth came out. He was mad I was a natural hustler. This envious snake went to my grandma and aunt Genie, telling them I was selling drugs. There are no words for how furious and frustrated I felt. First of all, what I did wasn't his business. Second, it wasn't even like he told for my well-being. He snitched because he wanted me to get in trouble to make himself feel better about how small of a man he was.

I held my piece because I knew I would have an opportunity to get even. The thing that pissed me off the most was while other people were selling crack and pills, I was only selling marijuana. And I know I'm saying 'only', but between my options of selling my body or cocaine, I felt marijuana was the best of any of the other evils.

My patience paid off. My best friend Katherine and I were walking the streets one day and we spotted him. We beat that ass. Snitches don't get off free where I'm from. Not even for minor stuff like this. But being the snitch he was, he couldn't even take the ass whipping like a grown man. He ran right back to my grandma. Upset, she and aunt Genie put me out. It hurt me she would go to such an extreme. I guess she felt I had disrespected an adult by putting my hands on them and her by selling drugs after being raised with her values.

I tried my best to be cool with this dude, knowing he was whack, for the sake of my mother and sister. The only reason his nosey ass found out I had paraphernalia was because we were watching a pay-per-view boxing match in my room and my aunt Lawanda asked for some weed. I retrieved a pinch from my stash and took it to her with him sitting right there. Mistake.

My exile found me living with my aunt Lawanda and Keisha for a few months. It suited me just fine. I loved being with Keisha. We did our normal. Hung out, ran the streets, sold a bit of this and that for change around the way and talked.

Eventually, my grandma wanted me back under her watchful eye. As my guardian, she realized if I got into anything in the streets, she would be the one to answer for it. I got the call at aunt Lawanda's to come home. It was time for me to go anyway. While I loved being around Keisha, and staying with my aunt Lawanda gave me a slightly different atmosphere, it wasn't all rainbows. Just like when Keisha and I were younger, aunt Lawanda still begged for money and weed. She never got in the habit of holding steady employment which made her rely heavily upon her boyfriend Al. But if the two of them didn't have enough scratch between them to make something work, the pressure was on whoever was around them they thought had some cash. With me staying there, she hoped to make me a walking ATM. Not my thing.

Keisha, on the other hand, constantly worked at various restaurants, so she was accustomed to her mother always asking her for money. Aunt Lawanda even asked us to get her food all the time instead of her simply cooking at the house. It was especially bad because Keisha worked at places with food, so in her mind it shouldn't have even been a big deal. And it might not have been except the fact she slept all day and watched Lifetime when her eyes were opened while the rest of us worked. So, no. I wasn't with indulging her or offering her the fruits of my labor when she had none of her own. I've never been an enabler and I don't believe in being one.

I can deal with a lot, but when you start begging...something about it sets me on edge. Once the word 'no' comes out of my mouth I expect the conversation to end. Especially with adults. If I could hustle and work my ass off, any able-bodied adult could. To top things off, the guilt others attempt to apply, assuming somehow it will make you feel obligated to take on their issues as your own is nauseating. I absolutely hate people thinking I owe them something. No doubt if I had nothing to offer she would have let me stay. But since that wasn't the case, that wasn't the case.

I stayed with Keisha a few more nights before going home. I don't think I would have hung around her as much if we were blood. She began lying a lot. To the point I thought she was mentally off. Growing up how we did it never surprised me to see the psychological effects people manifested. Without steady resources flowing through the house, she probably had to lie to get things she wanted or needed. We sure as hell stole. After a while, lying becomes as natural as breathing. You just say whatever comes to mind without thought.

I don't mean to come across judgmental or hypocritical, but I hate liars and lying to this day. I aim to be as authentic an individual as I can. This is likely why people flock to me. There is no guesswork. What you see is what you get. I'm direct. I like my garlic minced, not my words.

With Keisha, you weren't sure what you were getting. She would always be dating a guy if she knew I was dating someone. Little did she know, I knew most of them because, well, I knew almost everyone. She didn't have a boyfriend nearly half the time, and if she did, it wasn't the boy she said it was or it wasn't as serious as she led on. It would be a boy who she simply knew of. If I was doing it, she was doing it, whether she really was or not.

One commendable thing I recall about my cousin was how hard she worked as a teenager to help her mother out with bills. She could have been selfish, immature, and entitled like most our age, but she wasn't. Seeing her mother struggle, voluntarily, moved her to act. We were never afraid of work and always glad to make money. Last I heard she still works super hard to take care of them both.

I returned to my grandma, but the environment was heavy with disappointment. There was a short lecture about things that could and couldn't happen under her roof and what was expected from me. She kept it sweet and to the point. Ruth wasn't a nagger. I had created a distance between us with my behavior and decisions. Not that she didn't love me. Nothing I could do would ever change her love for me. My choices just hurt her. I didn't change anything though. I just tried to make sure it never got back to her.

I wasn't the most of her worries, unfortunately. At her age, I wish I had been. She didn't deserve anything else but the family still relied so heavily upon her. It was inconsiderate. My mom had been living with her on and off again. She found herself homeless and living in shelters more and more frequently.

Now, I was used to my mother's instability; and if she was the only one suffering the consequences I would've been fine. Except, Diamond was paying the price for her decisions. My baby sister. Ricky wasn't worth much; a leech. It was the only thing I could compare him with. He sucked everything out of my mom. She had a habit of falling for potential, like too many other women I've encountered, throwing their pearls to swine. She took men in their current state without any guarantee of progress.

To no one's surprise, Ricky showed zero ambition or ability to offer more than what he came with. Often unemployed, my mom would defend him and say

HE SUCKED EVERYTHING OUT OF MY MOM.

he was staying home to take care of Diamond while she worked. It made me sick to my stomach, knowing this grown ass man was sitting around while my mother worked. Eating food she worked to bring in the house, not contributing anything except dick to the house, watching my mom wear herself out to barely make it. What caliber of man could live this life?

Like she did with the ones before him, she begged the management at her jobs to hire him for almost any available position. Most of the time she was able to get it done. And Ricky, just like the ones before him, would accept the job and work a few weeks to appease her, then either quit or underperform to the point of termination. They insisted it was never their fault they couldn't stay employed.

I don't remember much more about him. I didn't care enough to be around them. Briefly, they stayed in an apartment up the street from Quilliams. With her so close, and my sister being there, I decided to give living with them a try. Mistake. My mom, thinking as many mom's do that their children don't deserve privacy, read my journal. Girlfriend got way more than she bargained for. I'm sure she expected to read a few juicy details about my innocent crushes on a boy or two. What she didn't anticipate was the wheres, whens, age differences, positions, and skills of my promiscuous exploits. Perhaps the frequency and quantity were much too. I kept a log of the boys, times, dates- all the details. Back then, I felt like a player for having them all under my belt. I thought I was in control and it showed me to be some type of progressive, mature female. In reality, I just didn't realize I was a whore.

When I found out she went through my stuff I lost my shit. There was nothing she could say to me as an excuse for indulging in my private memoirs and space. With neither of us backing down, the argument got physical quickly. I lived with my mom, Ricky, and Diamond for one week. Then it was over. After that, they got this super cute burnt orange Firebird coupe. It was fly as hell. I never got a chance to ride in it. Sadly they couldn't maintain it and it was gone within the next few times I saw them.

Every few weeks or months my mom and Diamond needed to stay with us. Ricky, he wasn't allowed. See, Ricky was dumb, but he liked to prop himself up and speak to my mom like she was the dumb one. Grandma wasn't about to subject herself to witnessing that in her own house. Plus, she'd be damned if she took care of a fully functioning grown man. He wouldn't be lounging around her house while my mom worked. That would be what caused my mom to take Diamond back into unfavorable conditions: guilt for leaving Ricky standing on his own two.

Nothing would have made them stay for a long period of time anyway. Where most grandparents love their grandchildren despite how they feel about the parents, my family didn't like Diamond as much as they disliked her father. My grandma and aunt Genie referred to him as slow. To be honest, and this is no compliment, he was one of the best men my mom ever had. With that in mind, imagine how worthless and vile the others had to have been.

It was rough for me. Diamond was my little sister, yet none of the family I grew up with wanted her around. I never understood why. Perhaps they resented her for being what bonded her father to my mother. They definitely hated the constant reminder she was of his existence. But none of it was her fault. She was a child and she really needed us to save her from both of them. I believe this played a part in the development of her character and behavior. As I resented my mother for not raising me, and slightly envied Diamond for having my mother active in her life, conversely Diamond likely resented the family for not offering the same relationships they had for me. I had the village. She had Deedee.

By 10th grade, I was tired of it all. I needed to move things along in my life in order to get to the next chapter. However, this couldn't be done without graduating. Anyone who knows me knows when I want something I make a foolproof plan to obtain it. If I come to you with a request or an idea, I've already worked the math and came to the desired end result. This greatly reduced my chances of having my request denied. I approached the principal of Cleveland Heights High with my agenda.

"I need to graduate a year early." There was no other way of saying it.

His face displayed his confusion. "There is no way for you to graduate early. It's impossible." It's discouraging to think back on how an educator immediately shot down an idea like mine without even considering the possibilities. But hey, that was Cleveland's educational system. I; however, wasn't discouraged by his apathy and laziness. Like I said, I already had a plan. I just needed him to sign off on it.

"It's possible." I laid out my thoroughly constructed agenda, which left him speechless. Clearly, no other student had ever come to him with such audacity and determination regarding their education.

"I need to graduate early in order to stay out of trouble. All I need is one year and your authorization to do so." I petitioned. I walked him through the year I needed. If I could take a zero period, which was a selection of courses offered an hour prior to the start of the school day, sacrifice my lunch, and take night school courses three times a week, I could achieve my goal. He immediately had concerns. In his mind, he heard me being in school from 7:30 a.m. to 7:30 p.m. without lunch and paying one hundred and fifty dollars per semester for night school. Directing his attention back to my game plan I advised I would eat on the go and had saved up money while working outside of basketball season to pay for night school. I overcame all of his objections. My detailed plan convinced him of my sincerity and resolve.

My family didn't buy it. Because of my past behavior, I lost their faith. It was more 'believe it when we see it' with them at this point. Which was cool. I was doing it for me and didn't need to prove myself to anyone else. This just underlined my need to graduate early due to the amount of trouble that led me to this place with them.

> **ANYONE WHO KNOWS ME KNOWS WHEN I WANT SOMETHING I MAKE A FOOLPROOF PLAN TO OBTAIN IT. IF I COME TO YOU WITH A REQUEST OR AN IDEA, I'VE ALREADY WORKED THE MATH AND CAME TO THE DESIRED END RESULT.**

I thank God for the support that bridged the gap for me. I had plenty of friends who fought my battles for me so I could stay out of trouble. Any mishap could have been a setback.

"Girl, you got this and we got you." They reminded me. They were right on both accounts.

That entire year I operated as a senior. I purchased senior pictures and memorabilia. When I presented my family with my graduation tickets they were floored. It started to look real to them. Maybe Ieshia was doing what she said she would. But college? No, surely she wasn't taking it that far. Unbeknownst to them, I already had.

Nine or ten colleges had received applications from me. What helped was the waiver of my application fees due to being classified as low income. Six of them accepted me and I chose Cleveland State in order to stay close to home. At 17-years-old I was scheduled to move into Viking Hall dorms located in downtown Cleveland off of Euclid Ave.

Two weeks before graduation, I participated in a two week internship at an insurance company. Still struggling with growth and character, I found a way to mess it up. No one found the gun I was alleged to possess, but girls in a rival group claimed I threatened them with one. This resulted in my vehicle being impounded and me being carted off to juvie. Here I was, two weeks from prom with eight pending cases. I hustled my butt off to get everything handled before then in an effort to not miss such a monumental occasion.

Here is where I will give credit to aunt Genie. Whenever family was in need she was right there making sure we had what we needed. I got an attorney immediately. Sure, he was a public defender, but he was the supervisor of the Public Defense office. Contrary to the reputation his subordinates earned for the department; he took my case seriously and pulled some strings to get me released just in time.

Genie rented a black Rolls Royce trimmed in gold with a chauffeur and I wore a powder pink dress with sparkles gifted by a friend. My original dress was forfeit since they couldn't get my measurements while I was in juvie. That was a thousand dollars gone from the down payment. My hair was in these fly, short curls because I was in a short hair phase in my life. To top it off, my date was my gay hair stylist, Astro Wade. Astro was the one who colored my hair all of the vivid, wild colors I experimented with throughout high school. I never held it against him that he severely burned my hair in a blonde experiment. I chalked it up to the game. He attended the school's cosmetology program so I was good being his guinea pig. Later we'll discuss how he betrayed me, a painful experience due to how far back we go, but not now.

Taking a gay guy to prom never crossed my mind as problematic. You knew there was nothing they would want from you at the end of the night. You could relax and enjoy prom for prom like any senior should. No added pressure. Anyway, most of the gay dudes I knew were super cool so prom was guaranteed to be a ball.

While prom itself was a blast, that night was even better. Yeah, I went with Astro, but I left with Fox. Fox's age made it inappropriate for him to be my prom date. It didn't bother him. He had no desire to be surrounded by a gang of excited, drunk high schoolers.

I never regretted my early graduation, just not being with my original scheduled class of '06. The class of '05 was cool and all, I had friends, but I went through the majority of my grades with the class of '06 and they were my people. For this reason, I don't attend reunions for either year. I don't feel as if I belong to either and never knew which to drop in on.

In 2006, besides the majority of my friends graduating, Ohio voters won a ban on smoking in public places. I thought it would be worse than it actually turned out. People acted like they were in hell each time they stepped into an establishment they could no longer smoke in. They threw fits, asking the owners to let them slide just one time. Nothing was like the first few winters when people weren't accustomed to being out in the cold. But they did it. True smokers will do anything for that hit.

It was a blessing in disguise for me. You could finally dance freely in the club without fear of bumping into the lit end of someone's cigarette or Black & Mild. Of course, you still had to make sure you didn't step on shoes, spill a drink, or get spilled on.

Even employers tightened up on their standards. Cleveland Clinic performed blood tests during the hiring process to disqualify smokers. It made the work environment more sanitary. Unfortunately, it did put people in a bind to find employment. Good thing for them, lower paying jobs always had lower standards for employment. There were still some good paying jobs smokers could get, they were just scarcer and more competitive than ever.

In 2008, we lost the home on Quilliams. The mortgage was difficult to stay current on. Grandma's pension of about a whopping seven hundred dollars per month wasn't enough for us to survive on with the cost of living steadily on the rise, especially in the suburbs. Since granddad's passing, uncle Terry was the main male figure in the house, beside Jamiel.

Jamiel's door stayed locked when he was gone and closed when he was home, which was rare. He worked a lot in his position as a bookkeeper with Advance Payroll. He earned a good living, but he and his money traveled most weekends. Work hard, play harder-a motto he lived by. As soon as his shift was over on Friday, he rushed home to freshen up, grab his pre-packed weekend bag, and headed out to spend his free days with Man, Linda, and Kenny. I remember Jamiel's devastation when Kenny passed away. He had AIDS or cancer, I don't know which. Jamiel was in a daze for days and wondered around monologuing in disbelief. Men don't tend to grieve like women. We are loud, open, and honest. Kenny had been a part of Jamiel's life for years. He buried his grieve and coped, but he lost a friend, and those close to him noticed the impact. I never knew much about his friends, but I heard of Kenny often.

Like aunt Genie, Jamiel powered his way through his careers from the ground up. He started at a local company called Blue Coral. People took note of how he helped businesses grow and maintain their books. If he wanted extra cash, as we all do from time to time, he did taxes on the side. I didn't even feel like he was part of the house at times. It was easy to forget he lived there. With the door closed or locked you just walked by and it blended into the wall after a while.

Not long after he moved into Quay 55, some super fancy condos on the water right before you hit downtown. Very few people could afford to live there. As a matter of fact, Lebron James and a couple of other Cavalier players stayed there, just to give you an example of the residents and their income. He stayed there for a short time then relocated to Houston, only to find himself back with aunt Genie in Cleveland. Being unsatisfied with his decision to return, he left again, this time for Miami and then Fort Lauderdale. I wish I knew what made him continue leaving, what he was running from or toward, but I didn't. What I do know is he wanted seclusion. For over two years he didn't returned a single text, call, or email I shot his way. He was avoiding his own family. I know some people have legit reasons for doing so, but nothing happened between us to put me on his bad side to my recollection.

Uncle Terry also held what we considered a great paying job at the time. He earned fourteen dollars an hour operating a tow motor. While the hourly rate may not have been substantial, he racked up more than forty hours most weeks, getting his money from the overtime. Not that the money went to good use. He struggled with an addiction to crack which robbed him of his pay every Friday and rendered him unreliable. Being high punctuated each weekend and he closed it out broke.

It saddened me that my grandma was losing another home. The good thing about it was, whatever decision they made from this point forward could be made without factoring me in. Hell, aunt Genie could have let my grandma live with her and alleviated the additional expense of another house. Terry could find somewhere for just himself. I decided not to dwell on it too much. They would handle it. I was headed to Viking Hall and that's all I needed to focus on. Me. Doing the right thing.

NEW BEGINNINGS

With everything that brought me to the point of graduation, I'm surprised I made it. Prostitution, jail, countless fights, promiscuity, losing family members, and the strained relationship between myself and my parents, how would I even focus on college? I didn't have a choice. In order to escape my past I had to learn from it. I had to enrich myself to elevate my life.

The vision I had for my future was larger than Cleveland could hold. I am eternally grateful for my upbringing. Because of it I can withstand anything. I'm glad I encountered every person I did. I've known the realest of the realest and can identify true friendship.

As I walked across the stage to receive my diploma, I heard my family screaming my name in the crowd for the first time. It was the sound I had been looking for all those years at track competitions, cheerleading events, and basketball games. It was all I ever wanted to hear; my village rooting for me in the midst of a major achievement. Today I had it. The girl in front of me got called and I watched as she shook the hand of the principal and waved into the crowd.

"Ieshia Jackson." All these years later. Remedial classes, honors classes, CAPS, suspensions, and now, my early graduation.

"Congratulations." The administration on stage smiled at me and shook my hand, delivering my diploma. I turned into the crowd to give a smile to the

> **PROSTITUTION, JAIL, COUNTLESS FIGHTS, PROMISCUITY, LOSING FAMILY MEMBERS, AND THE STRAINED RELATIONSHIP BETWEEN MYSELF AND MY PARENTS, HOW WOULD I EVEN FOCUS ON COLLEGE?**

camera I knew was taking my picture. With my diploma clutched in my hand, I stepped off of the stage and into what I prayed would be the most exciting chapter of my life.

MELVENIA

Ieshia entered my life when I was I transferred to Superior Elementary during 5th grade. I must have been eleven or twelve years old when my family relocated from the west side of Cleveland. Here was this popular basketball player and drill team member who everyone liked. Out of everyone I bumped into, she was the first to speak to me and make me feel welcome. We became fast friends and I joined the drill team with her. Our school couldn't afford team outfits so we wore red shirts and black pants to appear uniform. Our instructor, Ms. Britt, got us to perform in the MLK parade and took us to Six Flags. That was big for children who came from where we did.

Ieshia was unlike any other girl I ever met. She was addicted, and I mean addicted, to Pokemon. She collected the cards and kept them in a cd/dvd binder. I had never seen anyone with so many Pokemon cards or with so much passion for them. She also had a thing for Durango cowgirl boots. She wore them a lot. While everyone else was wearing shoes and sneaks, she looked like she was headed to a rodeo with her shirt, pants, belt, and boots.

As children, we had a ball. When her mother lived in Cleveland Heights we had sleepovers where we would just sit around and talk. From early on you could discern there was a strain on the relationship between them. It was a lot to actually see them interact with each other. Don't get me wrong, she loved her mother, but its translation was crippled by the pain of her mother's shortcomings.

Ieshia was so funny, not comedian funny, just in how she related to things and people. I loved being around her. Yet, there was a key to having a successful friendship with her. You have to know that she wasn't the one to call out because she would gladly serve you what you were asking for. Relationships with her were based on respect. She demanded it. You could not share the same space as her if you intended to disrespect her.

I remember a girl had stolen something from her, what it was or how she found out escapes me. What never left me was how she approached the unsuspecting girl on her way home from school and kicked her in the back when she spotted her leaning over a fence. The girl had no interest in fighting Ieshia, but she should have factored that in before taking something from her. Her tail got beat that day and no one could save her.

Another example of Ieshia's intolerance for drama was the thrashing she bestowed upon a boy named Angelo in one of our classes. We were being separated into groups for an assignment and he made a comment about how the groups were being formed. I never heard the comment. What I heard, and saw, was the rearranging of classroom furniture and Angelo getting what I am sure to this day is still one of the most vicious beat downs from a male or female in his life.

This was Ieshia. This was my friend. When she wasn't living with her mom she was with her great-grandma Alice, which was often. Upon meeting Alice you immediately understood where Ieshia got her no-nonsense attitude from. Just like Ieshia, she was a sweet old lady, until. Ieshia had a soft spot for animals. She had two huge ones I didn't bother trying to touch or play with. Anything Ieshia wanted, she got. She was a spoiled brat when she wanted to be. All she had to do was pout.

On days I chilled with her on Elberon, we would go straight upstairs and turn on music. If we wanted to be in the streets we would hook up with neighborhood children like Erica and a few others to catch the bus downtown and walk around or see a movie. Ieshia was a good friend and I have great memories from my childhood with her.

ELITHIA

I met my little cousin for the first time when I was 4-years-old. She was adorable. At 2-years-old she didn't have enough hair on her head to style, so my aunt DeeDee would crown her with headbands. She had the perfect face for it.

Ieshia didn't previously exist in my world. Her mom moved her to Las Vegas for a brief amount of time and they had just returned to Cleveland to stay at Ruth's house. Everyone in the family lived in the house on Elberon at some point, including my mother and me. The first introduction we had was when my uncle Jamiel picked me up and brought me over to get my gifts a few days after Christmas.

When I arrived, the sight of this tiny stranger surprised me. Who was she? I wondered about her as I opened my presents, side-eyeing her the entire time. Uncle Jamiel must have been watching both of us girls surveying the other because he scooped her up and walked her over.

"This is your cousin Keisha." The family rarely called me Elithia. He placed her on the floor beside me like the most fragile antique doll. "Tell her your name." He instructed me. We started playing the way almost any toddlers put together would. Ieshia had been given the most beautiful, pink Barbie dream house for Christmas. It was accompanied by a Barbie dream truck and a host of barbies to occupy it. I remember how tall the house was compared to her. I must have been looking at it too long, or standing too close to it, but before I knew it, Ieshia walked straight up to me and bite me in the face. That was the real introduction to who she was. I was hesitant of her from that point on.

Doll stayed our thing as girls. We took our barbies and baby dolls everywhere. They were our babies and we were their moms. We would spank them and love on them. When we got a few years older Ieshia would spend nights at my house. We'd grab blankets and build forts. My mom, LaWanda, never minded. She loved Ieshia. She let us take food into the fort since she knew we weren't likely to come out any time soon. Our fort time was spent talking, fantasizing, and sharing family gossip Ieshia knew. One of the biggest family mysteries to me at the time was uncle Terry. I never saw him much, but he lived at Ruth's. Ieshia informed me he worked all week, but was missing all weekend because he was a crack head and didn't give Ruth any money. Ieshia paid attention to everything and ear hustled. I didn't know how she knew he was a crack head at her age, so I asked my mother, only to find out it was true.

Ieshia shared the dreams she had for her future. At first, she wanted to be a lawyer like most children. Then she wanted to be a doctor which was replaced by the desire to be a singer. After that she went through a phase of wanting to be a teacher because she loved kids. But when she realized she didn't like them as much as she thought her dream changed again. These were my favorite memories with her.

When Deedee went back to work, Ruth kept Ieshia. I felt like we were always together and it may be due to this Ieshia grew possessive and protective of me. She was always feisty, but if you said something negative about or to me, Ieshia was fighting you. So, Ieshia fought often.

The neighborhoods we grew up in were slightly different. I lived in an apartment building and she lived in Ruth's house which was on a street saturated with children. She had more exposure to the streets and knew the rules, language, body language, and culture better than I did. This meant she picked up on vibes quickly.

I seldom knew what a fight was about. Ieshia took no shit and before a problem got a chance to really present itself, she was already physically solving it. We were a menacing duo, fighting up and down the block with anyone who had a problem with us. Eventually, someone would tell on us and Ruth would be on the porch calling for us to come home. We'd arrive, breathing labored, innocence plastered on our faces as if nothing happened.

If we weren't fighting, we were breaking open fire hydrants to indulge in the refreshing gush of water on scorching days. And don't let an ice cream truck come to the neighborhood. It would be stuck on one block for more than ten minutes while children went back and forth about which of their favorites they wanted, while others begged on porches for quarters and dollars from parents who didn't have it to spare. All of this to the cadence of a Master P or C-Murda hit. Those were our summers.

East Cleveland schools had very strict dress codes, but Ieshia had a fondness for a particular style. This was a set up for disaster. When she was six or seven, a teacher addressed her boots as a violation of the dress code. She warned her not to wear them to school again. Defiantly, Ieshia continued to wear the boots. In an attempt to resolve the issue, the teacher called Ruth and told her Ieshia couldn't wear the boots to school. While Ruth had been harsh on her own children, and even grandchildren, the great-grands got away with murder.

"Don't call my house about no damn shoes!" Was all the teacher received, and not a bit of what she expected. This was how she dealt with anyone who called her about us. "Don't call my damn phone about 'this' or 'that'."

Schools back then had paddles for disciplining students. Our family was very explicit in their stance that if there was a problem they were to be notified and they would do the disciplining, not the teachers. Ieshia knew this. The teacher decided to overstep her authority and struck Ieshia with the paddle for continuing to wear the boots. I would not have believed what happened next had I not witnessed it with my own eyes. Ieshia smacked the lady and pulled her hair. An epic brawl ensued with Ieshia winning.

My mom collected social security since she didn't work. Deedee was m.i.a a lot, so Ruth and Genie took care of us. There was no asking for five bucks. If we wanted money we made it.

We had two primary hustles: flowers and candy. The building I lived in had flowers around it we picked and sold to anyone we could get to purchase them. The candy was easier. Children loved candy. It was one of the things they bought the most with their pocket change. We walked into a Family Dollar or Dollar General with fifty to sixty dollars and doubled it by the end of the day after peddling it door to door in the apartment. Hustling was natural for us and we made a great team.

Yet, when she was on the scene, she was all I could have. It was hard to have friends in her presence. It seemed as if she picked a fight as soon as someone else came along who diverted my attention from her even in the slightest bit. One day we were playing with a bunch of kids from my building. They were all siblings, but I played with one of the girls in particular often when Ieshia wasn't over. All of a sudden Ieshia is calling the girl names and yanking on her hair. She was in full bully mode. It was so bad I pulled Ieshia to the side and asked her what her problem was. She paid me no mind. Finally, the girl's 16-year-old brother stepped to Ieshia and told her to leave his sister alone. Wrong move. That was it. Ieshia erupted into a frenzy and whooped his tail up and down the block. Here she was, 8-years-old punching, slapping, spitting, and jumping on him. I was paralyzed from the awe of this never-ending ass kicking. He was taller and heavier than her, but couldn't escape the assault until he removed himself entirely from her scope of vision.

For her 10th birthday, Ruth threw Ieshia a huge party in the downstairs area of the house. Ieshia had on a pretty white dress with blue and yellow flowers, white stockings and, you guessed it, white cowgirl boots. Her hair was always in box braids, but she wore them up in a ponytail with a few down in the back for the party. There was a large vanilla and chocolate swirl cake, with vanilla ice cream, pizza, enchiladas made by her mom, chips with dip, and soda. It was the perfect party, until it wasn't. The adults gathered everyone around the cake, lit the candles and advised it was time to sing 'Happy Birthday' to the birthday girl. Tamira must have forgotten whose day it was. She had started crying and Ieshia was telling her to be quiet so they could cut her cake. After a few irritated, yet peaceful requests, Ieshia got tired of it and smacked her dead in the mouth. Chaos erupted. Kids started arguing and fighting. I was confused. It was mayhem. I only saw stuff like this when I was with Ieshia.

Her father and members of his side of the family were in attendance and all the adults pinned money on her once things settled. From her neck down was nothing except dollars that had been pinned on. The party turned out fun despite the drama. She could fight you and keep it moving as if nothing ever happened. And it was her birthday. She wasn't going to be bothered by anyone on that of all days.

As if her aggressive, dominant personality wasn't enough, Ieshia also had a vindictive side. If you pissed her off and she didn't get you right then and there, trust and believe it was only a matter of time. Jamiel was very particular about how he dressed. It took him hours to get ready. Ieshia and I were in his room playing while he was in the bathroom putting on his final touches one day. She said something that irritated him, but I didn't catch it. The next thing I knew he was going off on her. She was visibly upset, so knowing her fits of rage, Jamiel and I left the room and were talking in the bathroom. About fifteen minutes later Jamiel returned to his room to get his soda, but as soon as he sipped it he spit it out. Come to find out, this chick poured half a bottle of nail polish remover into his soda. To this day he'll ask if we remember the time she tried to kill him.

The Ieshia you got depended on who you were to her. She would do anything for you if she loved and respected you. She loved coming up with ideas to cook breakfast for my mom and me when she spent the night. I wasn't used to making breakfast so it was fun when she did it, and of course, I helped. If she had something, she would share it. Ieshia took me with her to different school programs in the neighborhood and shared her lunches. She exposed me to things as a child I probably would not have experienced without her.

The older we got, the more adventurous. We went through a tomboy phase. They had woods behind the apartments I lived in that stretched for miles and miles. We explored them. We went places without adult supervision or permission, rode public buses to other cities and played with kids we didn't know. We were lucky we grew up in the time we did. It wouldn't be safe for today's children to do half of the things we did.

The one thing she wanted that money couldn't buy was a good relationship with her mother. Theirs was a strained dealing because she felt aunt Deedee didn't do enough for her. They had explosive arguments. I remember one time we went to the store to purchase candy, not steal it, and sold it for a profit. We were so proud of ourselves we showed the adults how much money we made when we got back to my apartment. Aunt Deedee wanted the money and it caused a massive scene.

"You don't talk back to me! You're my daughter." She yelled, and called her a bitch.

"I'm not a bitch! You're a bitch!" Silence filled the room. Everyone was stunned that at such a young age she was speaking to her mother like this. But this was Ieshia. She always took up for herself and wasn't willing to take shit from anyone, not even her mom. If you respected her, she respected you. Aunt Deedee had very little respect for her. Ieshia was constantly dismissing her from her presence when she felt attacked. Said she didn't want her around and would call the cops on her. There were periods when her mom would try by getting her and staying with Ruth or my mom, but it never lasted long. Ieshia just didn't want her around.

Aunt Deedee got pregnant when Ieshia was thirteen and it upset her tremendously. She demanded to know why she would have another baby when she didn't take care of the first one she had. I told her not to say things like that to her mother, but Ieshia refused to stop lecturing her on how irresponsible she was being. Her mother was the only member of the family she was indifferent towards. She loved everyone else because she felt as if she received their love in return. This was Ieshia.

MICHAEL EATON A.K.A. HERC

Born Michael Eaton, people who know me call me Herc. When I was six years old I fought a dude bigger than me. A dude who liked my older sister was out there watching it and saw me lift the kid up and slam him to the ground. From that point forward, people called me little Herc, short for Hercules. As I got older, they dropped the 'little' part from the name. Seems the name was meant for me anyway. I'm 5'7, averaging 215lbs. since I've worked out most of my life, much of which was spent behind bars.

When I wasn't incarcerated, I was running the streets with my partner Terry. I didn't know it at the time, but he was Deedee's uncle. In 1985 I came home from a three year stint for drug-related charges and robbery. I can't remember the details of what I was doing, but I was hanging around on 124th and Superior when I met Deedee.

We had a ball together. I was crazy about her and she was crazy about me. We spent most of our time getting high. We took rides to the park for picnics and the occasional dinner date, but for the most part, we just got high.

Deedee and I had been together about four years before Ieshia joined the party on January 20th, a week before my birthday on the 27th. I was elated. She was my 3rd daughter, though I was expecting a son. I had already had two daughters born two days apart in 1973, and one in 1980, all of which lived with their mothers in Cleveland. Deedee's doctor's appointments confirmed Ieshia would be a boy. A father wants at least one son to carry the family name. But it was all good. It just wasn't meant to be.

I watched my daughter enter the world through a cesarean birth. My heart was filled with so much joy and excitement: I had another child. The fact that my name isn't on the birth certificate is a mystery to me because I was there. I actually saw Ieshia before her mother did. I have no idea why my name isn't on my child's birth certificate. It has nothing to do with my affection for her or my desire to carry out the role as her father.

Deedee and I took Ieshia home to Alice's duplex and stayed on the vacant side. This is when things started falling apart. Deedee's family was very influential on how we raised Ieshia and the relationship between Regina, or Genie as they called her, and I was difficult. Regina had money. She landed a good job with the phone company straight out of high school and didn't have children or a husband to consider. I feel like this made her snobbish. I mean, this woman was something else. I tried to hang in there, but Deedee's family was always chiming in and it strained things between us. I left for Las Vegas when Ieshia was nine months old.

I hadn't been in Vegas for more than a few months before I found myself behind bars again. No matter where I went, it seemed as if I couldn't stay out of prison for the same mess. In the same way I couldn't leave prison or the streets alone, Deedee wouldn't leave me. She wanted to give us another try for Ieshia, and because she loved me. I was still incarcerated on June 14, 1989, when we got married. She relocated to Vegas with Ieshia and lived with my mother until she got on her feet. My family had moved there in the mid-'80s so she had a support system in place.

I was released again in 1992 and we lived in some apartments off of Sierra Vista. I wouldn't consider the neighborhood good or bad. There was a pool Ieshia was too young to really enjoy, but plenty of children around to play with. Even with that and my family being there, Deedee and I decided to head back to Cleveland a short six months later. It was only a matter of time before I got incarcerated again if we stayed. I was finding trouble or trouble was finding me at every turn. Prison was becoming a home away from home.

MICHAEL EATON A.K.A. HERC

My brother Cornell, who we called Meechie, had a few clothing stores and he allowed me to work for him when we returned. He was well off and self-made. Deedee and I tried to make it work. We were back on Elberon at Alice's where things were the same. Her family was determined to have the final say in what happened with Ieshia, Regina in particular. It's extremely difficult to parent and discipline your child when forces were working against you. The house had a basement you could use to travel between sides. If I said 'no' on something, Ieshia would dash over to the other side, get sympathy from her grandmother or aunt Regina, and whatever I said was overturned.

Alice Ruth and I got along for the most part. We may not have agreed on everything, but our relationship was nothing like the one I had with Regina. She despised me because I didn't live according to her standards. We had a huge falling out because she said I had nothing to offer Ieshia since I was poor. She wanted to raise my daughter her way. I advised her I had more to offer my daughter than she ever would since I had children, a wife, and love: three major things her life was missing which her money couldn't buy. I went further to say she would die an old maid and that I never saw a Brinks truck following a hearse. I gave her the option of either backing off or missing out on Ieshia's life. Regina's resentful nature exposed itself and she began poisoning Ieshia's mind against me. But like I said, my daughter is smart. She started deciphering things and noticed what was happening as she got older.

Between that and Deedee, it was over. By 1996 Deedee was off the hook, and I mean OFF! She was back on drugs and out of her mind. I couldn't handle it. We fell out for the last time and I left. Ieshia was 4-years-old. I assume Deedee divorced me in 2001, but I can't be sure about the date because, as usual, I was locked up and didn't get the notice.

Ieshia had always been a smart and caring child. She had a soft spot for animals and never hurt a person without cause. You got trouble from her if you came to her with it. She had that 'get up and go' about her that let you know she would be something special in life. When she had a goal, she focused on it until she figured it out.

After the separation, I tried to stay connected with her. When she began Rozelle elementary I walked her to school every day I could. I still battled with Regina trying to be the dominant force in her life. She was my child and I wasn't letting it happen without a fight. Eventually, she got Ieshia to follow most of her codes, which in part made her who she is today. The inner city is a rough place to grow up in and there is no shortage of peer pressure. Ieshia was able to stand strong because of the love, support, and family she had around her.

A year after she started school at Rozelle she got a pair of rottweilers. They were big, vicious, and the cause of the scare of my life when she was 5-years-old. The dogs loved Ieshia. A brother and sister lived up the street from the house on Elberon and chased Ieshia home all the time. It wasn't long before Iehsia was over it. One day during the summer I heard my daughter coming up the stairs crying. The girl and Ieshia had been fighting when the brother decided to jump in. I shot off the couch and noticed the brother and sister standing in front of the house. Before I could move another step Ieshia ordered her dogs, "Go get them!" They sprang for the children. My heart sank in my chest. I immediately had to call the dogs back. Thankfully they were obedient to me. All I could see were those two being torn apart before my eyes by my daughter's protectors. It was what they were here for and they were about to get busy doing their job. I spanked her for reacting out of anger then educated her on the dangers of their protective nature. Her dogs couldn't just be summoned as hit men to take care of her enemies. She would have to keep using her wits and fists.

The following year I allowed her aunt Regina to take her to Disney. Ieshia was spoiled. She was the first girl born into the family since her mother. And again, since Regina had money and no one else she was obligated to spend it on, she lavished it on Ieshia.

Over the years I watched my daughter become the product of her aunt Regina and her uncle, my brother, Cornell. They groomed her to handle business and finances well. Anyone who loved her and had a front row seat in her life was proud of what they saw in her: the makings of a success.

Sad to say, I started missing large pieces in her development. When Ieshia began junior high I began another prison sentence. A year or two of her life proceeded without me. I hated it. I've been trying ever since to make up for all the time I lost with her.

DENISE A.K.A DEEDEE

My life was good. I grew up surrounded by a loving and supportive family as an only child, in a home we owned in Cleveland. I had siblings, but they weren't raised with me. Life for me was carefree and I never paid the consequences for my actions.

For six years I worked at the Marriot near the airport. I used drugs and partied, but I was young without any responsibilities so, why not?

I met this really attractive man everyone called Herc, but his real name was Michael Eaton. He had grown up with my aunts and uncles, yet I hadn't seen him before. When my family found out I was seeing him, they warned me against it. It was too late. I was too far gone. He wined me, dined me, and kept me high. I wasn't going anywhere. Herc had a hustle I loved. I had my own money, which I never had to spend. We were always spending his. I was getting cars, mink coats, lobster dinners-leave for what? While it was just me and him, I felt like I was living my best life.

Then I got sick. I went to the emergency room and a blood test confirmed I was pregnant. I was disappointed. I didn't feel immediate joy. I was addicted to marijuana, crack, and alcohol. Knowing what that meant for my baby prevented the excitement most women experience when they find out they are pregnant. Instead, I felt more anxiety and fear. I didn't want this for my child. I felt so bad I turned myself in because I needed help to ensure I didn't harm her further.

I had stopped using cold turkey. When I told them, they advised me even that was harmful and potentially fatal to my baby because quitting abruptly deepens the addiction. I got monitored four times a week and it was hard because her father was still indulging and he was a bad influence. My favorite drinks: Jack Daniels, Bacardi Light, Heineken, Corona, and Moors Head were all off limits.

I wept a lot during my pregnancy. I could feel Ieshia balling up inside of me as if I were hurting her. I beat myself up a lot for the choices I made. Guilt ate me alive. If it weren't for the help I was receiving, I don't know how I would have made it through. Then there was my family, my greatest support system. Uncle Gregory, aunt Regina, and granddad William, who everyone called Buster, especially got me to the other side of things. By the time Ieshia was born, I was ready to be a mom.

Traffic delayed my granddad and he missed the actual birth. I only had Herc and Uncle Greg with me. Ieshia's positioning was not good for a natural birth. She was delivered by c-section. My first impression of Ieshia was that she was healthy. It was all I could pray for with the abundance of alcohol and drugs in my system when I conceived her and throughout the early stages of my pregnancy while they were weaning me off of marijuana and crack. I had learned a serious lesson. My body needed to be healthy because life comes from it and can be impacted by how I care for myself.

The need for support didn't end once she got here. She was my first child. I had no idea what I was doing. Although I had my own apartment, my family insisted we move into the house on Elberon. We did. I had been clean since my pregnancy and took on a job working for the dietary operations in a county nursing home.

Ieshia's father decided to relocate to Vegas shortly after she was born. I let him go at first. Then I missed him and followed. I had a decent relationship with his family, which allowed me to stay with his mother Isabell and sister Yvonne for the first two months while I got on my feet. I was always very particular about how I kept house, making it hard for me to live with anyone long. I got a job working in the dietary department for a hospital and moved across the street from it, allowing me to get to work easily.

Vegas was a good time in our lives for the most part. It was new and I did well for us. Ieshia stayed with her grandmother and aunt while I worked which made things convenient, except for one factor: D'jon. Yvonne's daughter Simone had a serious drug addiction. Nearly immediately after giving birth to D'jon Yvonne gained custody. The boy was a little younger than Ieshia, but knew he wasn't being raised by his parents. I had never met such an angry, bitter child in my life.

The first issue to come up with D'jon was he harassed Ieshia. He would pick at her incessantly, yet Yvonne refused to see the wrong in anything he did. She never chastised or disciplined him. The other problem was how he behaved when I called myself being nice enough to watch him while they went to the casino. Again, I'm particular about my house to the point of OCD. The child would ransack my house and write on the walls. This didn't work for me. Growing up, we knew to eat in the kitchen, not bounce around from room to room, and sit yo' ass down! I finally had to whoop his tail. Yvonne and I got into it behind the beating and I advised her to start taking him with her to the casino because he was too bad to watch. I despised him, and I know you shouldn't say something like that about a child, but I did. This damaged the relationship I had with the family and we stopped interacting for a while.

I began missing Cleveland. I found myself catching flights back home two or three times a month, just to stay for a day or two. My family was there and the distance became stressful. Relations were strained between Yvonne and I. It was time to go home.

Things changed between Ieshia's father and me. I no longer liked him, but I also couldn't escape him. I tried and failed. Having the cold steel of a 9mm pressed against your skull as you are forced into the trunk of a car destined for the bottom of a lake will do that to you. I was a mother. I had a child to live for so I stayed and endured the abuse. I dealt with the crazy. I got used to the stalking.

He wanted to remain active in Ieshia's life. I believed him, but his addiction started to make him volatile. He had the potential to be a danger to our child in my mind. He already proved to be a danger to me. The drugs weren't desirable to me anymore, but Herc didn't supply options, he supplied drugs. I lost trust in him and the threats didn't help. I had been clean for the first three years of my daughter's life. Her father made sure my sobriety came to an end. This is when things started falling apart between Ieshia and I.

She knew I was her mother, but my family raised her. I did what I could for her when I could. In my stead, my grandmother and Regina provided her with the best of things. I would have a place of my own from time to time. It would be a nice place with a stocked fridge, still I couldn't properly care for my child because I had a problem.

During the times I struggled with my addiction, Ieshia still respected me, just on a lower level because I wasn't the one nurturing her. I lost control of her once my family started fully caring for her and they put her against me. It was hurtful and made me bitter.

I tried once to regain control. The only reason I decided to step back was she was being well cared for. This had a negative impact on my relationship with my family, obviously. Tension was ever present. They were brainwashing my child.

As her mother, I wasn't ready to let go completely. I tried to do the right thing despite all their push back. I tried extremely hard and had been clean, but my family didn't believe me and kept her from me. Ieshia, being so young and caught in the middle, was oblivious to all of it. The pain started pushing me away. You don't know pain until you experience the child you carried in your body and birthed reject you.

They made sure money wasn't an issue when it came to her. Regina would go to Dillard's and buy her clothes and shoes, get her hair done, whatever she needed, or wanted, it didn't matter. Her prom dress alone cost a thousand dollars and was a custom order. Regina also sent her to prom in a luxury vehicle.

As soon as Ieshia was old enough to gain independence and venture out on her own, she did. Unlike other children, she didn't have a mind to just play. She liked accomplishing things. She got that from me. Ieshia became a hustler at an early age. Failure wasn't an option. Goals needed to be reached by any means necessary. Ieshia started selling candy in the neighborhood, then got into bake sales and selling hot dogs by 6-years-old. She could get money from family if she needed it, but she wanted her own. And Ieshia didn't spend what she made, she saved it. Her aim was to afford whatever she wanted. From the moment she could legally work she held two or three jobs.

There was no mistake about it; Ieshia was a leader from the beginning. Academics were the only priority above her hustles. I don't remember a time I wasn't proud of my daughter. No matter what her father or I put her through, she rose to the top like cream. That's my baby.

PRELUDE:
DEATH OF JACKSON

After graduating high school, I thought my life would take off into the clouds. I did the right thing. Cleveland State was to be the mechanism which propelled me into success. I needed to find my major, get an internship, and keep my G.P.A. at 4.0, minimum. I knew it was possible. So how did my plan go to shit?

After my days prostituting, I never thought I would use my body to earn money again. How did I allow Slim Goody to come to life? What lead to me being admitted to University Hospital? Was I as crazy as the other patients in the Psych ward they dumped me in?

Being from East Cleveland, you couldn't tell me I wasn't prepared for anything. The joke was on me, I wasn't. I don't know if you will ever be prepared for every situation thrown at you, regardless how rough and ruthless your upbringing. The universe has a way of surprising you, and it seems to enjoy outdoing itself. It definitely did a number on me.

Made in the USA
Monee, IL
15 January 2022